Exit Strategy

A practical guide to selling your business -
How to sell your business for the best price
and ride into the sunset.

By

Graham Watkins

The right of Graham Watkins to be identified as the author of the work has been asserted by him in accordance with the Copyright, Design and Patent Act 1988.

All rights are reserved. No part of this publication may be reproduced, stored in a retrieval system, or transmitted, in any form or by any means without the prior written permission of the author.

Copyright © 2006 Graham Watkins

All rights reserved.

ISBN-13: 978-1545416327
ISBN-10: 154541632X

Contents

Foreword — 1

Chapter 1 It's time to head for the hills. — 3
The different reasons for selling up - Personal objectives - Why an exit strategy is needed - When to start planning your exit - Dealing with confidentiality.

Chapter 2 Find the right trail. — 15
The alternative ways of selling a business - Public share offering - The London Stock Exchange – Amex - Ofex - Trade sale - Management buy out - Management buy in - Hybrid buy in – Acquisition - Voluntary liquidation - Compulsory liquidation.

Chapter 3 Head them off at the pass. — 25
How to prepare the business before you begin to market it - Cosmetic improvements that will make a good first impression - Operational improvements that will excite the buyer - Structural improvements that will add a wow factor - Legal improvements that will stop your buyer walking away from the deal - The fiddle problem.

Chapter 4 Hired guns. — 37
Why you need professional advisors - Where to find the good ones - The selection process to get the right ones for you - Negotiating fees - What your advisors should do for you - Avoiding conflicts of interest.

Chapter 5 How much is it worth?   **53**

Why you need a valuation of the business - The different methods used - Valuing minority shareholdings - The conditions needed for an open market - Defining a fair price - Net asset value - Comparison with a similar company - Using return on investment to calculate value - The value of goodwill.

Chapter 6 Howdy stranger.   **65**

How to begin to market your company - The advantages and drawbacks of advertising - Creating a buyer shortlist - Who to include and avoid - Why you need to keep control - Creating initial sales particulars that will attract the right buyer - Making the approach - Why you need confidentiality agreements and how they work - What to include in a stunning business profile - Dealing with unusual visitors.

Chapter 7 Let's deal.   **81**

Negotiating the deal – How to prepare for the negotiation – Establishing your objectives – Building in flexibility – The right place to conduct the negotiations – How to conduct the negotiation – Why you use the 'we' word – Listing the issues – Making the agenda work for you – Refining issues to your advantage – When to use your fall back positions – Communicating with your team during the negotiations – How to deal with nasty surprises – Adding value to the deal with concessions – How to avoid overplaying your position – Heads of Agreement and what they do.

Chapter 8 Here comes the posse. 99
Due diligence – where the term comes from – What it means – Why the buyer conducts due diligence – The right way to answer questions – How to use your lawyer – Keeping copies – The benefits of full disclosure - The questions that will get asked – What the auditors are looking for – How to avoid a clash of culture – The fairness of due diligence.

Chapter 9 Back at the ranch. 111
Keeping the business going – The buyer is watching – How to keep your staff motivated – Ways to reduce the effects of stress – Preparing a cover story – Why you should make no structural changes – Avoiding short term gains – Your role as a caretaker.

Chapter 10 It's a contract Jim, but not as we know it. 119
Purchase / Share Sale Agreements – What they are – How they protect the buyer – The structure of a Share Sale Agreement – What it includes – Definitions – Consideration – Completion – Completion accounts – Escrow accounts – Warranties and representations – Tax covenants – Restrictive covenants – Understanding the jargon – Negotiating through the lawyers – Using other lines of communication.

Chapter 11 We meet at dusk. 131
The completion meeting – What it is for – Who attends – Where it takes place – Timing – A

stressful climax – Getting your paperwork ready – What happens during the completion meeting – How to make it a formality – What happens to the money.

Chapter 12 Riding into the sunset.   **141**
Dealing with announcements – Telling the staff – Handing over control – Consultancy agreements – Stocktaking – Completion accounts – Honouring your obligations – What next.

Exit Strategy

Foreword

When my wife and I decided to sell our business in 2000 we had no idea what was involved. Scouring libraries for good advice on the subject and talking to professionals we quickly realised what a big project selling up is and that there is very little written on the subject that the entrepreneur, who is not a book worm, can turn to for help.

If, like me, you have a short attention span and prefer to make decisions while things are happening you will appreciate why many business owners make a mess of the last big part of their career, selling up. To do the job properly takes time, in our case three years from making the decision to finally walking away. During those three years we made a lot of mistakes and went through a meteoric learning curve. There were a number of false starts, dashed hopes and tears on more than one occasion.

We were fortunate in the choices of our financial and legal advisors. Their calm and reason helped keep things in perspective when everything seemed to be going wrong. I am indebted to my wife for helping me stay focussed throughout, to Phil Oliver of UHY Hacker Young Chartered Accountants and Robert Cawdron of Acton's Solicitors for having the patience to explain the complex issues we were dealing with and for offering good advice that enabled us to work our way slowly to a sale which, I believe, was satisfactory for all sides involved.

This book is not a record of the sale of our business; indeed the confidentiality agreement, our purchasers insisted on, does not allow it. Instead it is my views, based on personal experience, of what is involved in selling a company. I do not pretend 'Exit Strategy' is a textbook. Others far more qualified than me have already written mighty tomes on the subject and these are available to the scholars and academics for debate. The audience I have written for are those of us who are involved in owning and building businesses; people that get on and do things, the backbone of UK Plc.

I should acknowledge and thank my friend Dave Simkins FCCA and Phil Oliver, Senior Partner at UHY Hacker Young for their comments and suggestions regarding the content of this book together with the input of my cousin Graham Watkins and his wife Avis. Their gentle corrections of my appalling grammar helped teach me where to stick my commas.

Since I do not claim to be an expert, I recommend that you take professional advice before making any important decisions about selling a business.

If, as you read this book, you learn something that helps you sell your business successfully I will be pleased. I hope you enjoy the read. I certainly enjoyed writing it.

Graham Watkins
Garnlwyd

Exit Strategy

1   It's time to head for the hills.

When asked about capitalism, the American philosopher, Norman O. Brown said, 'The dynamics of capitalism is postponement of enjoyment to the constantly postponed future.'

It took me a while to digest but what he was saying was, 'If you are running a business it's all consuming and takes over your life.' And of course he's right.

But, one day you will be leaving your company. It may be tomorrow, next month or years in the future, but that day will come. Disposing of the company will be your last act of entrepreneurship related to the business. The finality of the transaction will be daunting and exciting, probably leading on to a major change in lifestyle. It will almost certainly be the biggest single deal you will ever make. Exiting your business can, if done properly, set you and your family up for life, lead on to other exciting projects and leave a business run by enthusiastic motivated staff.

Get it wrong and you will find yourself losing out. The business that has been your livelihood and the primary driving force in your life for years may turn out to be worthless, a paper shell you have built around yourself. Disposing of it can become a nightmare, leaving you with very little to show for all the years of work you have done. In the worst case you may find yourself liquidating the assets to pay the creditors and discover that the bank wants the shirt off your back. The difference between these extremes is influenced by numerous factors. Many are covered in other business help books. Marketing, finance, human relations, staff motivation, production control are just a few examples of areas where you will have to know your stuff if you want to succeed. Even if you have learned and applied all of these skills, it is unlikely that you will experience a clean, profitable and enjoyable exit unless you have worked out how it is going to happen. Without a thorough and detailed exit plan you will not get the best price and terms for you company.

Have you ever thought about how you are going to exit your business? Probably not because, you see, like death, entrepreneurs don't talk about leaving and that's a big mistake.

It may seem strange but, like death, the idea of planning how you leave your business is rarely considered until the time has come for it to actually happen. Why this is so is not difficult to understand when you remember that, in order to run a successful company you, the business leader, have to be ruthlessly focussed on the business itself. You must be positive; totally motivated towards developing the business and making it achieve its full potential. Start thinking about leaving or retiring and your positive focus is gone, your level of enthusiasm reduced. How can you lead your troops when you are thinking of deserting them? It's safer, you tell yourself, to concentrate on the job in hand and get on with driving the business forwards. Tomorrow will take care of itself, you reason. But will it?

The question is, when should you start thinking about how you are going to leave your business?

At whatever stage you are in the development of your company you will already have some idea of what you are trying to achieve in the long run. Even before you start your business, you will have long-term goals - making lots of money, the big boat or retiring in the sun. However, in the start up phase of any enterprise short-term goals such as getting the next order or finding a supplier for tomorrows production are paramount. They demand immediate attention. Planning your exit is the last thing on your mind but, even so, the seeds motivating you towards the end of your career will already exist. One day, you will have told yourself, you will spend more time with your family, play more golf and see more of the world. While you may dream, it is unlikely that you will be thinking seriously about leaving and almost certain that you will have devoted no time to start planning how to do so.

As your company thrives and grows, the idea of retiring, financially secure, and leaving the legacy of a successful business behind will still be in the back of your mind but the busy owner manager finds little time to consider the distant future. You are far too occupied with staff problems, dealing with customers and all the other issues affecting a dynamic operation.

It is only when the time comes to pass the leader's baton on to someone else that most entrepreneurs start to work out how to exit cleanly and achieve the best reward for themselves and their family.

But what if there is no exit plan?

In the worst cases the exit strategy is never planned. The consequence of having no strategy can be disastrous. Take, for example, the owner of a successful service company with no immediate plan to retire and who had given no serious thought to eventually standing down. His business was his life. Everything else came a poor second until the unexpected happened and, at the age of 55, he suffered a massive heart attack and died. He left behind a tightly run business, led from the front. There was no obvious second in command to step up and take control of the company.

The dead man's son, who had never been involved in the concern, until now, ends up abandoning his own career and taking over to protect, the family's main asset, the business. The family decide to negotiate a hasty sale of the company. The sons' inexperience means he makes some bad decisions. Sales slip, good customers walk away and staff become frightened. Some key staff leave, taking key clients with them. Eventually the business is sold, but at a substantial discount to its previous market value.

Exit Strategy

The financial loss and the stress the family and staff experienced would not have happened if the owner of the business had displayed the foresight to build an exit strategy into his overall business plan. From this story, it is apparent that exit planning is something that you should start years before the time comes for you to hand over the keys and walk away.

And here's another reason for thinking about your exit now, right this minute. A good exit plan will help you drive your company to greater success.

Far from being a de-motivator, understanding and developing your own exit strategy will help you focus on issues that will strengthen the company, making it more efficient and capable of superior performance. Look, for instance, at the area of succession within the company. Most buyers will want to purchase a business that stands on its own feet. That means if you, the existing owner, disappear the company will continue to trade without problems and that the important decisions can still be make by someone experienced and competent. This may not be just one person. Often it is a management team. Part of your exit planning therefore, is to build a team that can operate when you are not there. Without it, as we have seen in our example of the service company, there is a risk of collapse and a reduction of value to any prospective buyer. How does this produce superior performance? It's simple. By building a management team you are strengthening the business, harnessing the people within the company and inviting them to help you achieve even more. The focus this style of management adds to your business will bring significant improvements in performance potential as well as generate new ideas and energy.

There is another advantage in building a team ready for your exit. In doing so, you create a layer of staff who can take responsibility, leaving you with the benefit that you can delegate more. Delegation of power and responsibility will in turn release you from an enormous amount of pressure, the enemy of all entrepreneurs, and make the daily job of running your business easier.

Here's a strange thing. Planning and grooming my business for the day I would be departing changed the way I ran the company and preparing the business for my exit actually helped you stay longer.

Question most independent business people about their working life and they will complain about their workload and the conflicting pressures involved in getting things done. They don't have the time to get the sales, run the factory, deal with red tape and build a management team all at the same time. You may well recognise this complaint and agree with it. If you do, you are in the same position as most of your peers, but not all. There are exceptions. Not all small company directors have this type of workload. They are the business leaders who are successful and yet make it look easy. They do not display the signs of stress or manic energy guaranteed to burn out before the end of the race.

These are the business leaders who have, often, already started to plan their exit route. They have already passed on many of their responsibilities. They will make it in the long run and retire, riding happily into the sunset, taking the highest reward with them while leaving a strong working team behind to carry the business on into the future.

So why leave?

Regardless of what type of business you are running, unless you intend to drop down in harness, you will have to leave at some point. The reasons for walking away are as varied as the types of businesses there are. They do however fall into five main categories and combination of categories. These are: -

The first and most obvious is Retirement.
The time may have come when you want to slow down and liquidate your business, your key asset, to secure your financial future and enjoy doing very little.

The second is It's time for a change.
You may have become bored with your business and want to try something totally different. Selling up for a good price will generate the capital you need to start again.

The third Ill health.
You may not want to leave but realise your health is suffering. The stress or long hours may be getting to you.

The fourth Outside opportunity.
You may have an unexpected offer from another company. Perhaps a competitor or supplier has decided that they want your business, that it will add value to their own operation.

And lastly the fifth Outside threat.

All products and markets operate in cycles. The business you started may be in a declining sector or have unfashionable products. Possibly, the time has come to sell and get out while the business still has value. You may even have the bailiffs knocking on the front door.

Scan through these five reasons for leaving again and you will see that they are, for most entrepreneurs, in order of preference. Would you prefer to ride off into the sunset with the boardroom silver, a big pension and smiles all round or fight the receiver for any assets left after the liquidation and destruction of your life's work?

Let's consider the first reason, retirement.

In a perfect world, retirement is the part of your life when you have the money, the health and the time to do what you want. The constraints of running a busy company and being on parade before staff, suppliers and customers are gone. But why sell up to retire? Some do not. Instead they give the job to a successor and step back while retaining some ownership and interest in the business. For most small business owners this is not possible. The idea of moving from the driving seat into the back seat is fraught with dangers. You can end up keeping the worry without having the direct control to take action. If you interfere, your actions can subvert the new director's leadership and authority.

Perhaps you do not have someone suitable in your family or interested in taking over. You may be unwilling to hand control of your business to an outsider while retaining the risk of it all going wrong.

Another important factor in making your retirement decision is financial. Selling the company is often necessary to release the value of the business to fund your future lifestyle. Under present tax rules, this is an efficient way of getting your hands on the money without handing a large chunk of the cash to the government.

As a result in most cases where the owner manager wants to retire, the best course of action is to sell up and make a clean break from the business. That way, you leave the responsibility and the worry behind while taking the money to enjoy or invest somewhere more secure.

The world is constantly changing and, for you it might be time for a change

We are being told increasingly that no job is for life and there is no rule that you have to stay running one business for your entire career. If you don't enjoy going to work, it may be time to explore another type of business or occupation altogether. Selling up will release you from the existing one and provide you with the money to start again. Like any other reason for selling, you will want the best price possible and an effective exit strategy will help you achieve it.

The third reason for exiting a business Ill health is a tough one.

Like the American philosopher Norman Brown said, running a business can be bad for your health. The long working hours, people problems, financial worries, snatched lunches and neglect of our own well being all contribute to the problem. Early signs include heavy drinking, excess weight, poor sleeping patterns and high blood pressure. These should all be taken seriously and action taken to find the causes so they can be dealt with before they become more serious. If this includes selling the business you should not hesitate. It is time to implement your exit strategy.

Outside opportunities the fourth reason for getting out is interesting.

It does wonders for your morale and confidence when you are approached with an offer to buy your company. Somebody wants your business. They think it is worth paying good money for. It may be the quick way to retire or to become part of something bigger and even more exciting. If you are approached, someone else has taken the initiative. The correct way to turn the proposition to your advantage is to have your exit plan already in place. It will clarify the key issues for you including your asking price and will act as a blueprint, enabling you to negotiate a profitable transaction, one where you, not your prospective buyer, are in control.

Lastly and perhaps most unpleasantly comes the last reason for exiting. An outside threats one which might destroy the business you have put your life and soul into.

Exit Strategy

Trading a business in serious difficulties or one that is failing can be a crushing experience. If you own, as well as run, the company the pressure is far worse since if it goes under you lose not only your job but your savings and even your family home may also be on the line. Fortunately, there are early signs of impending failure which, read and understood correctly, can be acted on. Marketing can be modified, products changed and savings made. If however, the problem is serious and outside your control it may well be time to sell. You probably do not have an effective exit plan. Even if you do, it may be too late to implement it unless you can buy time, rethink you business model and rebuilt your company. Remember to include an exit strategy in your next business plan.

So, you see, now is the time to start planning for the future so that you do walk away with the boardroom silver and still have the shirt on your back.

Planning and implementing a good exit strategy from your business takes time. In many cases it involves several years work. The sooner you make a start on this important project in your company the quicker you will feel its benefits both as you continue to trade and also eventually when the time comes for you to leave. Don't put it off until tomorrow. Tomorrow may be too late. Start thinking about the issues that will increase the worth of your business and make it easier to sell, today.

Before we go any further I must ask, can you keep a secret? – You can? OK let's talk for a moment about confidentiality.

Selling a business is far more complex than most owner managers realise when they start the process. The temptation to discuss and share ideas is attractive and here lies a real danger. If you do talk to the wrong people, you run the risk of sending confusing messages and damaging your business. Tell your staff that you are training them as part of your exit strategy and they will imagine you will be gone next week. Panic and confusion will follow. Mention to your suppliers that you have had your company valued and they may take fright, lowering your credit limit or looking for another route to market. Tell your bank manager that he may be losing your account, when you are taken over, and who knows how he may react.

The right time for sharing information with all the parties concerned will depend on the nature and the details of your business sale. Do not tell anyone that you are preparing an exit plan, or have started to implement one, until you have worked out how to deal with any repercussions. Your ideas and plans should remain confidential until you are ready to share your news. Tell no one except those who have to know and who you can trust not to repeat the secret. That will include far fewer people than you imagine. The subject of confidentiality and how to deal with keeping the secret will be covered in more detail later in this book.

2 Finding the right trail.

The businessman James Oppenheim wrote. The foolish man seeks happiness in the distance; the wise grows it under his feet. Was he talking about his business, the way he ran it and how he planned to leave? I bet he was and, what's more, he hit the nail right on the head.

There are a variety of ways of selling a company and before deciding which method to use you should take some time to think through your reasons for selling and how you want your personal circumstances to change once the business is no longer yours. This may sound strange but understanding the future lifestyle you want to achieve will help you decide the route you use to take your business to market.

It may be that you would like to continue running your company in the future while at the same time selling a major interest in it. Possibly you want to exit slowly over a period of time, reducing your involvement in stages. On the other hand, you may prefer to grab the cash, hand the keys to the new owner, show them where the kettle is and walk out the front door without looking back.

These are all possible outcomes and achieving the outcome you want will be influenced on how you sell the business. Let's consider them.

The first and perhaps most ambitious is floating your company.

Floating a company involves making a public offering of the shares in a private company, turning it into a public company quoted on a stock market. It is the most high profile way of selling all or part of your business and can give you a personal cash windfall while at the same time leaving you remaining in control of your company. This is a good option if you want to leave over a period of time but there are some drawbacks.

The three markets for trading company shares in the UK are the London Stock Exchange Main Market, The Alternative Investment Market (AIM) and Ofex now succeeded but the electronic share trading platform Plus Markets Group. The main market is designed for larger trading concerns usually exceeding £30 million capitalisation. Cost of entry to this market is high and involves rigorous testing and documentation. There are over 2 million limited companies listed at Company House but only 2500 whose shares are traded in the main London market and about 500 of these are foreign companies. Less than 1% of limited liability companies registered in the UK are listed in the main market and it would not

Exit Strategy

normally be an appropriate avenue to use for an exit strategy.

The AIM and Plus are both smaller markets created to cater for the demand from less substantial companies wanting a public listing for their shares. Rules of entry and reporting are more relaxed than the main market but are still far more onerous than those required from private companies.

The process of turning a private company into a public one involves making an 'Initial Public Offering' {IPO} and is done using a raft of advisors, brokers, lawyers and reporting accountants. The IPO is made to private and institutional investors and is usually underwritten by an institutional investor to ensure its success. The procedure involves a lot of work and it is the most expensive way of selling a business. Even in the smaller markets, the cost of making a public offering of shares will be £350,000 or more depending on the size of the floatation. Clearly the size of your business is a consideration before electing to go this way.

The advantages of listing include the ability to raise capital finance for expansion, a higher profile for the company and the opportunity for the existing owners to cash in part or possibly all of their investment. Expanding the capital base of a business as it grows is a more common reason for listing as a public company.

The drawbacks of floating a company are the increased regulation and reporting involved both during flotation and afterwards, loss of overall control and the cost. In addition, there is a risk that the future market in the shares may not be big enough to enable the existing owners to sell the remainder of their shares because there is no demand in the marketplace for them. In effect, the existing owner gets locked into the business. There are also market rules, different in each market, relating to how soon existing shareholders can divest themselves of additional shares after the floatation and, since investors are looking for continuity, the existing directors can find themselves contractually committed to staying with the company. Without that commitment the floatation may not succeed.

The time commitment can also be substantial and the chief executive who moves his company from the private to the publicly quoted sector can expect to spend 25% of working time dealing with the floatation and the increased corporate governance that follows.

The timing of your floatation is critical since the markets are volatile. An attractive and desirable investment for investors one week can quickly become a liability as the mood of the market changes. This is particularly true of faddish sectors like 'dot-com' companies where demand for new listing reaches epic proportions before the bubble burst and many rising stars reveal themselves as grossly overvalued. The ideal time to offer your company to the market is when the economy is booming, the stock market is rising, your business sector is fashionable and your own business is peaking in terms of its profitability and performance. It is not an easy trick to get right. Before embarking on a floatation, take detailed professional advice. For a great many businesses a public listing is not the appropriate mechanism to use as part of an exit strategy.

The next option is a trade sale.

Disposal of the company via a trade sale is the main alternative to taking the business public. It is a simpler process than flotation and is generally less expensive. There are a number of alternatives covered by the description 'trade sale', each appropriate for different circumstances and dependent on the size and nature of the business.

The first of these is a management buy out - MBO.

The Management Buy Out, as its name suggests, involves an existing manager or managers within the company purchasing the business from the owners using funding from a variety of sources. These may include personal savings, bank borrowing, business angels and venture capital funding. Other funds a buyer may use are junk bonds and so called 'alphabet loans' both used by larger buyers to give added leverage and delay capital repayment. The nature of the funds and the way the funding is structured will depend on the detail of the transaction and the objectives of the different parties who come together to buy the business. Venture capitalists, for example, may be looking for a short-term capital return and plan to float the company and sell their shares within a few years while the incoming owner managers may have longer term objectives. When negotiating the sales of your business to your own management team care needs to be taken to avoid any conflict of interest on the part of the buyers. Remember, they are conversant with your company, warts and all, and as prospective buyers will be after the best deal for themselves.

A trade sale might also involve a management buy in - MBI.

In the case of the Management Buy In, a group comprising of an outside management team and their financial backers buys the business. Because the management team does not have prior experience within the business, it is a higher risk proposition for the buyers and most venture capitalists will need a very strong case before they will consider investing. They will want to see significant potential for growth or a nag that they can easily grow into a race winner before selling on. Venture capital providers sometimes have proven managers that they use on a serial basis as they move from one project to the next. As a result, your initial negotiations may start with the financial backers before the new management team appears on the scène.

Alternatively it might be a Hybrid 'buy in / management buy out' – BIMBO.

The higher risk associated with a management buy in has led to deals being put together where external managers are bought in to supplement and strengthen the existing managing team buying the business. The 'buy in / management buy out' or BIMBO gives the buyers the benefit of experience within the concern and adds the extra management skills that due diligence identifies as being necessary. Using this combination to lead the company forward can significantly reduce the buyer's risks.

A simpler trade sale is where your business is purchased by another company.

Selling the shares in your company to another business has, from the vendor's point of view, a similar outcome to any of the above transactions. You part with ownership of your business, take the money and exit, sometimes after a handover or consultancy period. In the case of acquisition by a larger concern, there is no venture capitalist in the picture and the incoming owners may have plans involving integration with their existing operations. By merging or acquiring businesses they may gain economies of scale, domination of a market sector or some other benefit that adds value to the whole. Publicly quoted companies benefit from the purchase of private companies since they can re-value them at a higher value after buying and generate capital growth. It may seem unfair but the perceptions of a businesses value are higher if it is a quoted company.

Of course there are other ways to leave including a voluntary liquidation.

Normally, a trading business is worth more than the value of its underlying assets and it is preferable to sell as a going concern where future potential profits add value to the business. Intangibles like goodwill, customer databases, intellectual property rights, a loyal workforce and a recognisable trading name all add to the worth of a going concern. However, there may be circumstances where no interested buyer can be identified and winding up the business becomes the only practical alternative. Sudden ill health of the owner may force the company to stop trading leaving no option but to sell the assets such as stock, vehicles, equipment and premises to pay creditors. This distressed sales of assets invariably results in the assets being sold below their market value. Before the owner can take his money out, all other creditors have to be paid. The list of creditors has a strict order of preference with the ones at the top being paid first. These are generally the Inland Revenue together with Customs and Excise followed by any bank borrowing or overdrafts, the redundant staff and other unsecured creditors. The shareholders stand right at the back of the queue.

The shareholders may end up with nothing and, if they have given personal guarantees, can find they owe money to the creditors. It is no accident that banks ask for the comfort of personal guarantees and second charges on the homes of company directors.

If you choose a voluntary liquidation, you need to plan ahead and prepare the business. Reducing stock, collecting unpaid accounts and slimming down the operation will help to make the process simpler and easier. Once your debtors learn that you are closing down they will find plenty of excuses for either not paying at all or negotiating a discount. Suppliers also need treating with care. Tell them before you need to and you risk losing your trading credit. They may even take fright, close your account and demand immediate payment. The effect of one key supplier over-reacting can damage the business and even bring it down in an uncontrolled way. Staff who are losing their jobs deserve some compassion and redundancies should be treated correctly and sympathetically. There is no point in adding complications by creating claims for unfair dismissal.

The most damaging way out is, of course, compulsory liquidation.

Unpaid creditors can force the winding up of a company. These may be the Revenue and Customs, the bank or a supplier to the business. Trade suppliers are normally unsecured creditors and do not usually issue winding up petitions since they are less confident about receiving payment when the receiver has taken his cut and paid off the secured creditors. There is often insufficient money in the pot to pay all the creditors. More usually it is the tax authorities or the bank that cause the company to cease trading. When this happens, the running of the business is put in the hands of an 'Official Receiver' appointed by the creditors. His job is to examine the company's affairs and make trading decisions on behalf of the creditors. He can continue to trade as a business and try to sell the company as a going concern or close it down. The official receiver controls all company assets and reports to a meeting to which all creditors are invited.

At the creditors meeting, the controlling directors are required to face the creditors and can be questioned about their past running of the business. The creditors then take a vote deciding how the liquidation is to proceed. During a compulsory liquidation the shareholders have no control and the fees charged by the receiver will reduce any money they may receive from the winding up. It is unusual for shareholders to receive a payout following a compulsory liquidation. Forget the boardroom silver, that's gone to pay creditors.

There may be a temptation to hide assets or pay off the bank and hide some cash, leaving the unsecured creditors taking all the pain. If you value your reputation it is not a good idea. In cases where company directors can be shown to have acted improperly they can become personally liable for the debts of the business even if no personal guarantees have been given. As well as becoming liable for outstanding money, a dishonest director can be barred from being a company director in future.

The official receiver also has a duty to report cases of directors acting dishonestly or fraudulently.

So what is the most popular way out?

It depends very much on the type and size of company but a trade sale of the business is the most popular and common way of disposing of a business. It is easier and cheaper than a flotation and avoids the destruction of liquidation. Selling through a trade sale also avoids the volatility of the stock market although timing remains important if the outgoing owner is to get a good price for the business and leave quickly and cleanly. Making a trade sale exit is the option we will concentrate on in the coming chapters.

Exit Strategy

3 *Head them off at the pass.*

Winston Churchill. the British war leader said, 'Let our advance worrying become advance thinking and planning.'

Great advice for anyone in business.
Before you can sell your business for the best price, there is a considerable amount of preparation that you need to do prior to hanging the 'for sale' sign up outside. Prospective buyers will prefer to buy a business where everything looks good and there are no problems. A smart looking, profitable operation will attract the serious buyer but that, on its own, is not enough to achieve your objective.

Not only must the business look good and perform on paper, it should have no hidden problems or undesirable secrets. Even if you have got the attention of serious buyers, once they discover something unpleasant within the business your sale is jeopardised. At the very least the buyers will use the issue as a negotiating tool to lower your price and if the problem is perceived as serious it can become a deal breaker, causing them to walk away. The result of the deal falling apart mid way is unnecessary cost, frustration, distraction from running the company and possibly damage to the business itself.

The answer to unforeseen problems is to search for them in advance and sort them out. By clearing away the debris and any hidden traps, you make the business more saleable and gain a tactical advantage that will help you during the sales negotiation. You would not normally try to sell a house without making it look its best, perhaps by sprucing up the kitchen and tidying up the garden. If there were a leak in the roof you would repair it since the buyer's survey would discover the fault and cause doubts about the rest of the house. The leaking roof could even cause the buyer to pull out. The same principles apply to the sale of your business but, in the case of a company, the issues are far more numerous and complex than those involved in selling a house. The buyer will not have one surveyor looking for problems like leaking roofs; - he will have a whole team of them and they will be crawling into every corner of your company.

Possibly the easiest improvement is cosmetic.

The saying, 'you don't get a second chance to make a good first impression' is true and particularly appropriate when you are selling a business. The first time a prospective buyer visits your company he will be making value judgments. Are the premises modern, clean and well presented? Did the reception look inviting? Was the signage professional and did the company literature on display look smart? If the

Exit Strategy

answer is "no", you are already starting to drop off the radar as a possible acquisition. The fact that your company may be a fantastic goldmine with great potential becomes irrelevant since the buyer may not bother to look any further than your shabby front office. You can lose the sale before the purchaser has even looked at the business in detail.

Scruffy buildings should be decorated and tired receptions smartened up with new furniture and fittings. A lick of paint and a tidy up of the flowerbed may be all that is needed outside. But if rather more work is required it is worth investing a little time and money to get the appearance right. Don't leave it until later. By then it may be too late.

First impressions do not end in your reception area. The rest of the premises are equally as important. If you have a factory, it should be clean with gangways clearly marked and work in progress neat and tidy. Rubbish should be cleared away. Safety equipment and signs need to be clearly visible. The same applies to your offices. Set a standard for your staff. Make them clear their desks each night before they go home and make space available for stowing personal effects away so they are not cluttering up the place.

Prospective purchasers will examine the literature you are using to promote your products and services. It must set the right tone. In these days of desktop publishing there is no excuse for second-rate literature. Remember you are selling image and it should be just right.

Do you have a dress code in your company? Smart and appropriate clothing helps make the operation look professional. The uniform is a great way of raising a company profile and it is no surprise that most leading companies have adopted corporate uniforms for their staff. If you want your business to project the right image, follow their example.

Let's look now at the operational parts of the business which will affect its saleability.

Moving on from first impressions to areas that will impinge on the efficiency of the business, areas that buyers will want to examine in detail. They will be looking for pointers explaining how the business works and potential problems that will affect any purchasing decision. Is the business profitable? A business that has reported a steady growth in profit over several years is far more attractive than one that has struggled to perform consistently. If you are planning to sell in a couple of years time, now is when you should be driving profit up and showing the increase clearly in the audited accounts. Your business plan should be up to date and include strategies for marketing, human resources and production as well as the usual numbers.

Do you have a written health and safety policy and have appropriate risk assessments been produced for the business? If there are any disputes with suppliers, now is the time to sort them out before you become involved in any sales negotiation. It may be that there are quality problems or customer complaints outstanding. Get them resolved ahead of marketing your company. As you deal with each issue, document what the problem was and the action that you are taking to resolve it. During the sales process, a professional buyer and his advisors will be quizzing you about all these issues. Demonstrating that you already know about any problem they raise and confidently showing how it is being handled look professional and is a good way to dispel any negative reaction. On the other hand, if you cannot answer the questions, doubts will surface on the buying side. To some eyes, your company may begin to look like it is being run as a 'by the seat of its pants' outfit!

Is your business Structurally sound?

A key part of your company that any buyer will want to explore is its internal structure. Fundamentally, will it still operate when you are gone or are you essential to the business? Will the whole operation fall apart without your presence? If it would, the purchasers may not complete the transaction. They will want to feel confident that the existing staff, possibly with a new management team bolted on, can continue to run the business when you have departed. To help this happen you need to have built a viable team structure that will stand on its own feet.

Look at your management team. If you don't have one, warning bells should already be ringing. While you may be willing to stay on, supporting the business as a consultant or technical advisor, you will not maximise the value of the business without a supporting team in place. Develop key members of your staff by teaching them aspects of your own job. Have team meetings and discuss the trading issues that affect the business. If necessary, make someone else in the team chair the meeting and be prepared for the team to take extra responsibility as they grow into more senior roles. Mentor your managers as they develop and allow them to make mistakes.

Training should not stop with key staff. Everyone employed in the company should be moving forwards. The 'Investors in People' programme can provide the right momentum and serve as an attractive badge to show potential buyers. Developing a training plan for the business can also be a good stand-alone project for one of your managers to undertake.

Private companies are sometimes treated as the personal fiefdom of the owners and the line between private and business assets can become blurred. There may be personal assets being used in the business that are not on the balance sheet or assets owned by the business that you wish to keep after the business has been sold. These matters need tidying up before you put the company on the market. Leaving them unresolved until the middle of the sales process is a mistake that will confuse matters and discourage your buyers.

Take a fresh look at your assets. Are they correctly valued for today's market or has your depreciation created an unrealistic position? Get premises surveyed and an up to date valuation made. It is worth the cost and will make your balance sheet a more worthwhile working document.

If there are old debts that you are never going to collect, write them off. There is no point carrying them forward and expecting a buyer to accept them at face value. They won't!

If your business is in the middle of any long-term project involving change, aim to bring it to a conclusion prior to offering the company for sale. No buyer will be happy about buying a company in the middle of a period of major change. To be attractive, the business needs to be stable and ready for the new owners to make their own changes to it in the future.

An area that many entrepreneurs fall down on is the legality of the business! Here it is sometimes surprisingly small things that can, and will, trip you up.

Now is the time to make sure your business is completely legal and above reproach. Audited accounts need to be up to date and filed at Company House on time. Details of Directors and their share holdings should be registered correctly. Your company tax affairs should be in order and paid on time. This includes Corporation Tax, VAT, Income Tax, National Insurance and any other duties that you may owe. With the introduction of employee self-assessment, the Revenue and Customs have more resources available to conduct tax investigations and no potential owner wants to become embroiled in one, particularly, as a result of something that has happened before they bought the business. Consequently, prudent potential buyers will go through your business tax affairs with a fine toothcomb.

It may be that the business and possibly you yourself have recently been the subject of an investigation by the tax authorities. If you have, so much the better, for two reasons. Firstly, it is less likely that the tax inspectors will return in the near future and, secondly, if there was anything untoward, it will probably already have been discovered and dealt with. This can be a critical area of concern and the buyer will nearly always insist on the seller indemnifying against any past tax liabilities that come to light after the sale is completed.

Is all your computer software licensed? Many companies add workstations to their network using existing software without purchasing the extra licence required. If you are in this position or have bootleg or beta test software on your computers, get it removed or buy the correct licences.

Do you have written terms and conditions of sale? You should have, and your purchaser will be asking to see them. Now is the time to make sure that your trading names and any logos that you use are properly registered to your business or that you have the legal right to use them. If there are any patent issues or restrictive covenants imposed by your suppliers that you are flouting, get them sorted out.

It is possible that your business is in dispute with someone, maybe a customer, a supplier or an ex-member of staff. If you can, settle the disagreement and remember to keep a written record of the details. Possibly you are unable to resolve the argument. If this is the position, make sure the matter is properly documented and that you can explain the best and

Exit Strategy

worst possible outcomes. Buyers will ask about any recent or outstanding conflicts involving the business.

Every employee should have a written contract of employment and a job description. Employment law is becoming more complex and potentially more expensive if you get it wrong. Employment tribunals are full of companies making simple mistakes that have cost them dearly. Personnel records need to be up to date. Areas of potential discrimination need tidying up. If you have people doing the same job but on different wage rates where the difference cannot be justified get it put right.

Another area to look at is your disciplinary procedure. Does it comply with current regulations? If not, bring your disciplinary rulebook up to date and include it in your company handbook together with your drink and drugs policy, internet policy, anti discrimination policy and all the other policies that demonstrate the professionalism of your company.

Are all your employees qualified for their jobs? You may have a warehouseman who has no licence but uses the forklift truck. If you do, send him on a course. If your land is contaminated, get it cleaned up and tested so you are able to prove the site is not a problem. Environmental issues are becoming a serious matter and if there is any doubt about waste contamination, even if a previous owner was responsible years ago, get the site checked and keep the surveyors report. Your buyer will almost certainly be asking questions and you will need to be able to answer them.

Check your Memorandum and Articles of Association to make sure you can proceed with a sale. If there are any shareholders agreements giving pre-emption rights or restrictions on transfer of shares, these will need resolving. Minority shareholders have legal rights. If you own more than 90% of the shares, you can give a buyer the absolute authority to buy the remaining shares in the business even if the other shareholders object. By owning 75% or more of the shares, you have the right to liquidate the business or put it up for sale but you do not have the ability to force the remaining shareholders to sell their stake in the business.

A shareholder with more than 50% but less than 75% of the shares has day to day control of the business but is not in a position to put the business up for sale or liquidate it without the support of the other shareholders and a minority shareholder with 25% or more of the shares can stop the company being sold or put into liquidation.

Many potential buyers will not want to purchase a business with minority shareholders who may become a nuisance in the future. The best solution is to remove the minority shareholders, buying them out, before you begin marketing the company and before they are aware that you intend to sell the business. If they think you are going to put the business up for sale, the minority shareholders will expect, and probably get, a higher price for their shares.

Make sure your share register, the minutes of statutory meetings and your returns to Companies

Exit Strategy

House are all up to date and correct. If they are wrong you may encounter problems during the sale process.

By now you may be thinking that there are an awful lot of potential issues to address. You are right and the ones described so far are by no means a comprehensive list. Fortunately, you will almost certainly already have a large number of them covered and there will be others that are irrelevant to your company. The advantage of grooming the company so that you can satisfactorily answer most, or preferably all, of a purchaser's enquiries is significant. It will make your business appear a professional and more attractive proposition. Do the job correctly and you will have a substantially improved negotiating position as the sale progresses. Preparing the business properly can make a big difference to the final price you get for the business.

Finally while we are discussing legal issues what about the fiddles!

One area that few entrepreneurs will discuss in public is the effect of the black economy on their business. Some owner managers of smaller companies will admit privately however that part of their business is done 'off ledger' for cash. The main advantage of dealing in cash is that the payment of tax can be avoided. Not paying Vat, Income Tax, National Insurance and Corporation Tax substantially increases the profit the business owner keeps for himself.

You may be tempted to under declare turnover or profit but it is a mistake. The valuation of your company will, in part, be calculated on its historic profitability. By not declaring all of your profits in the audited accounts you are reducing the apparent value of the business you are trying to sell. Even worse, the multiplier that is applied to the annual profit to arrive at a valuation means that there is little real financial advantage in avoiding the payment tax. Other common accounting tricks used to reduce tax liabilities include undervaluing stock and work in progress or treating the purchase of capital items as revenue expenditure. These also need addressing, as does using company money to fund private expenditure. It may mean that you may pay more tax for a couple of years before you sell but the money paid in extra tax is a good investment that will repay itself in the form of a higher selling price for the business.

Not only is there a direct financial advantage in having clean and complete accounts but any buyer who discovers cash deals are taking place will start to wonder what other nasty things are happening in the business that they don't know about.

Another serious consideration is that tax investigators take a dim view of dishonest business owners. Not paying your tax is illegal and the tax authorities are adept at identifying businesses that fiddle accounts to reduce their tax burden.

4   Hired guns.

A man who represents himself has a fool for a client and a fool for a lawyer. I'm not entirely sure where this quotation came from but it highlights a key issue when selling a business.

There are plenty of experts happy to act for you and help you sell your business. Many wear smart suits, drive luxurious cars and know the right words to use when they want to impress. If you are an entrepreneur who likes to get on and do it your-self, your natural reaction will probably be to keep well away from the experts. These people know how to charge; they cost money and since it is your money, it is tempting to try and sell the business yourself. After all, you will have had years of experience in your industry and know far more about your company and the market it operates in than any consultant or self proclaimed expert you have ever meet.

Perhaps you have had a bad experience with a consultant who borrowed your watch, told you the time, and sent you a bill for the privilege of learning what you already knew before sending the watch back with a broken hour hand. If you have, the idea of bringing in outside advisors to help you with the sale of your company may be unwelcome but this is one occasion when it is better to stand back and let others act for you. True, it will cost you money but the cost will be small compared to the cost of getting the whole process wrong.

Indeed, for some exit strategies you have no choice in the matter. To float your company on the AIM, for example, you are required to employ a specialist advisor from an approved list. 'No advisor, no flotation' is the rule and even after flotation you are obliged to retain the services of this specialist advisor. Without him on your pay-role your shares are suspended and cannot be traded. Regardless of legal compulsion there are other sound reasons for finding and hiring the right people to help you drive through the sale of your company.

Remember the size of the transaction, probably the biggest you will ever make. This is no time to learn the ropes as you go along. Learning through your mistakes is not an option. You need to plug into the knowledge, experience and skills that the right intermediaries can offer.

Exit Strategy

Forget any prejudices you may have about 'consultants'. Put your emotions to one side.

Your company will be a prized possession built up through many years of hard work and sacrifice. The emotional connection you have to the business means that you are too close to the product, your company, to act as a professional salesman. Instead, you need an intermediary to act for you who is not emotionally involved, one who can operate objectively under pressure and negotiate the sale on your behalf. His objectivity and calm will help guide you through the decision making that you will find necessary without getting hung up or taking things personally. By acting as a calming influence your intermediary smooth the process and make it easier to negotiate the hurdles when they appear.

In chapter one I mentioned confidentiality.

Handling a complex sales negotiation involves frequent contacts with potential buyers and their advisors. The sales process is a major undertaking and almost impossible to conduct from your premises without everyone wondering what is going on. Buyers, financial backers, bankers, accountants, surveyors and sundry other parties all quickly get involved and if you are negotiating with several possible purchasers the problem gets even bigger. The stream of strange visitors, phone calls and questions being asked about how the business works can quickly distract staff and create suspicion, damaging morale at a time when you need the business performing at its best. Because the intermediary operates from his own offices he is able to keep your direct contact with the buyers to a minimum and conducting the sale away from your business makes it easier to control the process and maintain confidentiality until it is the right time to make any announcement.

Your hired guns are your contacts and will insulate the business from damage.

In order to sell your business you need to be able to find potential buyers. Finding the right contacts and talking to them is the only way you can begin the sales process. Without making the right connections the sale will not happen. Suppliers and competitors are one obvious source of potential buyers and you may already have produced a list of possible suitors worth approaching before you engage your intermediaries. But is the list big enough? Will it give you the best price for your company and the best terms? The answer is almost certainly 'no' since you do not have the knowledge or the experience to find the best buyer. You need help from someone who knows the market. By bringing in good outside advisors you will dramatically expand the list of potential purchasers capable and interested in buying your company. Your intermediaries will have their own contacts. They will know venture capitalists looking for target companies to buy, owners of larger businesses who want to expand through acquisition and management teams looking for the right business to buy into.

Choosing an intermediary with the right stature adds value to your proposition since your company is now backed by his reputation. His contacts will know that he is professional and works with the right type of companies. He will have dealt with these people before and his name will open doors that you do not even know exist.

Good hired guns bring experience to the table; negotiating and sales expertise you need.

From the start you need an intermediary who is proactive and prepared to get his hands dirty. A good intermediary is willing to search for potential buyers, write the sales agreements, conduct negotiations, field awkward issues and work hard throughout to achieve the best possible deal. As the sale develops, issues will arise that, if dealt with incorrectly, can become a deal breaker or result in the offer price being reduced. Your intermediary will be aware of these potential issues before you are and his negotiating expertise will help you keep the deal going in the direction you want. The people who are going to buy your company will employ an aggressive strategy to negotiate a good deal. Their organisation may well be bigger than yours and may probably have done this before. You need a team on your side that can match their skills and experience.

Lastly delegating the job to hired guns gives you time and keeps the emotional stress of selling up at arm's length.

Running a successful business is a full time job demanding total commitment. So is selling one. Both activities take a great deal of time and energy and it is unlikely that you have the time available to do both properly. Using intermediaries to sell the business enables you to remain in the background and concentrate on running the business while your selling team gets on with selling the company. From looking for a buyer to completing the transaction can take several months and the owner manager rarely has the spare time or mental stamina to take on the project of selling the business and keeping the operation performing properly.

So, what intermediaries do I need?

The types of intermediaries you employ will depend on the route you choose to take the business to market. Since the main stock market is an unlikely target as part of an exit strategy we can ignore it but the intermediaries needed to enter the smaller markets are worth discussing.

First of all let's consider a flotation.

To list on the AIM you will need the following specialist advisors. A 'Nominated Advisor' - sometimes called a nomad - is a compulsory requirement. The nomad has to be selected from a list approved by the market and must stay with the company after it is listed. If your nominated advisor leaves or is fired, your shares are suspended and cannot be traded until a replacement is appointed. The nomad's job is to manage the flotation, instruct the other advisors, draft documents, ensure the rules are followed and act as a conduit between the city and the company. The cost of this advisor can range between £100,000 and £150,000 or more if the floatation is a complex one.

Exit Strategy

You will also need an accountant experienced in preparing suitable accounts and who has a profile that creates investor confidence. The accountant's numbers are a significant part of the proposition and they will also be dealing with due diligence, taxation, the issuing of shares, management accounting and corporate governance. Depending on the size of the company the accountant will cost between £20,000 and £500,000.

As well as the legal requirement to have a nomad you are also required to have a broker. Sometimes these two roles are combined. The broker's function is to create a market for the shares to private investors and institutions. For the float to succeed the broker must have good contacts and the right experience. The cost of a competent broker will be between £100,000 and £150,000. In addition there will be an annual retainer to pay of about £30,000.

The corporate lawyer's role is to draft the legal documents and advise you regarding compliance with the laws and regulations relating to becoming a public company. It is a specialist role that cannot be undertaken by a high street solicitor. Expect the cost of a corporate lawyer to range from £35,000 to £100,000.

For the float to succeed, the profile of the company has to be raised, making it attractive to potential investors and easier to attract funding. The PR consultant's role during the initial public offering is to promote the floatation with accuracy. He does this through journalists in the investment media and by going direct to the institutions. The PR campaign will cost in the region of £25,000 to £40,000.

Other advisors and experts may need to be drafted in depending on circumstances including surveyors, valuers and specialists needed where the appropriate knowledge does not already exist in your team. All costs quoted are indicative and will vary depending on the market and the quality of the people you select. A close look should be taken at the overall cost when considering the suitability of an IPO.

The expenditure for entering other alternative markets is broadly the same as the AIM and the decision about which market is appropriate is one that should only be taken after listening to detailed professional advice.

What if you are planning a trade sale?

A trade sale is less complex than making an IPO but you still need to recruit the right intermediaries for the reasons already discussed. The key intermediary comes with a range of possible titles - investment banker, broker, chartered accountant, merger practitioner to name a few. Regardless of his title, the job is the same, i.e. to drive the sale process along. He is your agent and acts on your behalf throughout the transaction. As an agent his role is to advise and act on your instructions. He is not a decision maker and should seek instruction from you when any decisions have to be taken.

The selling of a company occurs in a number of distinct phases and your agent's job is different during each stage.

Exit Strategy

First they should - Prepare short sale particulars for the company. Identify potential acquirers, circulate the particulars, follow up and generate interest.

Second - Issue confidentiality letters to interested potential buyers. To prepare a detailed business profile and circulate it to the interested parties after they have signed confidentiality letters.

Third - Conduct negotiations with potential acquirers and agree indicative offers for the business.

Fourth - Provide assistance to the seller during the buyers due diligence exercises.

Fifth - Give detailed advice on purchase and sale agreements. Liaise with legal and other advisors. Advise on warranties and the implications of terms and conditions in the sale documentation. Attend meetings with your lawyers and generally to drive the deal forwards.

And finally sixth - To attend the completion meeting and complete the sale.

From this list, it is apparent that your agent is the front man during the whole process and his job is critical to the successful marketing of your company. Many selling agents operate on a fee system that is contingent on making a successful sale but may ask for a fixed fee in the event of you withdrawing before a sale is finalised. They also usually ask for the right to represent you on an exclusive basis for a fixed period of time. It's a reasonable condition when you consider the amount of speculative work they are undertaking. Fees payable will be in the range of 2% to 5% of the sale value achieved. For a company selling for £2 million, the agent would take between £40,000 and £100,000 in commission.

The second key intermediary, the lawyer, does not get directly involved until an indicative offer is on the table. His roles are to ensure the deal is done properly and to protect your position. Selling a business is a complex transaction and this is not a job for a general solicitor. You need a specialist corporate lawyer on your team who has the right experience in dealing with the issues affecting the sale and who is supported in his practice by other specialist lawyers - a commercial property lawyer for example - who can be used if needed. The corporate lawyer does the following jobs for you: -

First - Prepares a range of legal documents including the confidentiality letter, share sale agreement, purchase agreement, warranties and indemnities, consultancy agreements, letters of disclosure, official meeting minutes and stock transfer forms.
Second - Advises the seller on the implications of all the documents concerning the sales transaction.
Third - Replies to the legal enquiries from the purchaser's lawyers.
Fourth - Negotiates the final draft of the legal documents.
Fifth - Attends the completion meeting, completing the legal requirements of the transaction and collects

Exit Strategy

the consideration (money) from the new owner's lawyers.

Unlike agents, lawyers rarely work on a contingent fee basis. They are not willing to depend on a satisfactory sale for getting paid. Part of their role is to give you sound advice and that may even include suggesting that you walk away from an offer that is on the table. The dynamic is that while your agent should be driving the sale forward your lawyer is checking all the details, sounding a note of caution from time to time and applying the brake to make sure the sale is not rushed into without being properly prepared. Corporate lawyers usually charge by the hour but will offer to work on a fixed fee basis in some cases. Anticipate a cost of £20,000 to £30,000 in legal fees for selling a £2 million company.

A number of financial documents will need to be prepared before, during and after the company sale has been finalised. The agent you appoint to handle the sale can, if he is an accountant, take on the role of accounting advisor. The advantages of combining the jobs include having a smaller group conducting the transaction, lower costs and accounts that are designed to sell the business. Accounts and financial reports that need preparing include introductory numbers for the short sales particulars, the accounts for the detailed business profile and the completion accounts. Completion accounts are normally prepared by the purchasers accountants after the completion meeting but your own accountant will be required to check them before they are agreed by both the buyers and sellers. The completion accounts are similar to normal audited accounts and confirm the final price being paid for the business. The cost of these and the other financial reports will depend on the size and complexity of the company.

What are the right characteristics for your hired guns?

Having established the roles and responsibilities of your intermediaries you need to consider what their characteristics are and the sort of people you want to do the different jobs. You will need to establish a good relationship with your advisors and must feel comfortable working with them. Look for intermediaries who are on your wavelength and easy to talk to. They need to be receptive and understand your points of view. You are the client and should expect them to make the effort to explain complexities without talking down to you. The agent should be enthusiastic, a salesman with the right experience, someone who wants to get things done. This is not a role for a procrastinator or a reserved individual. Your lawyer also needs to communicate on your level. Avoid corporate lawyers who pose or suggest your deal is a little on the small side for them. Ideally, you want a younger lawyer who has experience but is still building a name for himself, who still has something to prove. Perhaps he is a junior partner in a larger law firm.

It is important to remember that you are putting together a team that will need to work closely together in numerous meetings. You will all need to be on the same wavelength and able to present a unified face to your buyers team. If you feel uncomfortable with any of the intermediaries you are considering, move on and look for someone else.

The next question is where to find your intermediaries?

The first member of your team will be your agent. Start by looking for accounting practices that specialise in handling the sale of companies. Accounting firms frequently mail-shot offering free seminars for entrepreneurs considering selling up. Go along to these meetings and listen to what they have to say. If you have any contacts that have recently sold out, give them a call and have a chat. They will understand the need for keeping your ideas confidential and may be able to recommend someone that they have used. Your Chamber of Commerce might also be able to help. They will almost certainly have suitable bigger accounting firms as members. The chief executive of the Chamber is likely to be on first name terms with the senior partners. Other possible starting points for your search are listed in the appendix. While yellow page list accountants in droves, most will not have the right experience and be unsuitable for this type of work.

The same areas that will produce your sales agent will reveal a suitable lawyer. When you have found your agent, ask him for a few suggestions for a corporate lawyer he thinks will do a good job. He wants the project to be a success and will want to work with someone reliable, who will do a good job. It is worth paying close attention to his suggestions.

OK now you have some possible hired guns to consider. What next?

Once you have a short list of candidates, invite them for interview. If any refuse to take part in your interviewing, cross them off your list. Insist that the person who will be dealing with the details of your transaction attends. That may sound strange but, with bigger practices, a senior partner can show up to win your business and then turn the job over to a junior employee who is totally unsuitable in some way. You interview a thrusting, assertive leader and end up with a bean counter afraid of his own shadow. During the interviews, ask the candidates to explain how they operate and get them to tell you what will be involved in selling your company. Act as if you know very little and let them expand your knowledge. As they present their case for winning your business you will begin to form an opinion about their suitability. Enquire about their fee structure and if it is negotiable. Towards the end of the meeting, ask for a written proposal together with at least three references from satisfied clients who they have sold similar sized companies for.

The question of references is important since it will demonstrate suitable experience and give you the opportunity to talk to their past or existing clients. Completed deals are the only proof that a candidate can do the job for you. Conclude the meeting without making any commitment to use them. If necessary you can tell them you still have someone else to interview.

Exit Strategy

Professional intermediaries will understand the reasons you are taking your time and part of the meeting will involve them sizing you and your business up. They will be asking you questions about the business and your reasons for putting it on the market. If you have unrealistic ideas about the value of the business or how it will be sold they may even decline to tender for the work.

During the interviews you will have rejected some of the applicants and unsatisfactory written proposals will eliminate others. By now you should be down to two or three possible agents who all appear suitable. At this stage, start phoning the references they have provided. The candidates will have spoken to their referees asking permission to use their names and priming them to expect your call. During each conversation you need to probe with detailed questions about how their own transactions progressed, how they got on with their intermediary, how he dealt with problems and about the quality of the advice he offered. It is worthwhile to prepare your questions in advance and make notes of the answers during each conversation. Your notes will help you make a final selection.

In the event that your final candidates do not meet the standard you expect, reject them all and start the selection process again. It is better to spend the extra time finding the right person than accepting second best. You are only going to sell your business once and 'second best' will cost you money.

While you're recruiting your hired guns, watch out for any conflicts of interest.

One scenario where you need to exercise caution is where a selling agent who has a buyer interested in your company approaches you. It is tempting to think of going through the sale using his services. You don't have to find your own agent and saving the cost of employing one may sound a good idea. It isn't. Do not rely on the services of the approaching sales agent since he is working for the buyer and will be looking after the buyer's interests not yours. Even in this situation it is prudent to recruit your own agent preventing any conflict of interest occurring.

Exit Strategy

5 *How much is my business worth?*

***The value of a business is the price someone is prepared to pay for it in an open market.
A valuation is an opinion – nothing more.***

How do you value a private company? The answer depends on a number of variables. Are you looking for the value of the whole company or a proportion of the shares? If you want to establish a value for some of the shares, the valuation method used will vary depending on how many are involved. The holder of a controlling interest will have his shares valued one way while a minority shareholder, one that does not control the business, will find the shares are valued using a different method, giving a lower value per share. The resulting lower value reflects the lack of control the minority shareholder has in the business.

As well as valuing different sizes of share holdings using different methods there are alternative ways to value depending on the type of business being examined. Complex rules apply to valuing shares in different circumstances and plenty of case law has been generated to settle disputes and establish precedent.

The value of any business changes all the time. In the case of a publicly quoted company, there is an open market for the shares and their prices move up or down, driven by the demand. As a result, you can see the value of shares in a public company at any time. With a private company, there is no open market for the shares and it is more difficult to establish a value.

When shares in a private company change hands, they are subject to scrutiny by the tax authorities. The Inland Revenue has a Shares Valuation Division based in Nottingham. Its main task is to make tax assessments on share transfers. The Shares Valuation Division can request to see your valuation with supporting evidence and frequently challenge valuation assumptions.

There are accepted methods and conventions for valuing a business but the key to a sound valuation is to consider that the business, or its parts if it is going to be broken up, is sold in an open market.

In an open market, the buyer and seller must be willing to undertake the transaction. If the vendor is forced to dispose of the company, say by creditors, the sale is not being made in an open market and a lower price may well result. Selling in an open market requires every possible purchaser to have an opportunity to buy. If the number of buyers is limited, possibly to competitors or close acquaintances, a lower price will be achieved. Conversely, if there are more prospective purchasers, a higher price will be obtained.

A perfect open market would be an auction attended by the entire population. That way, every possible purchaser would have a chance to bid. It's an impractical idea and clearly there needs to be some compromise position between the entire population and a few friends. To market your company effectively, you need to know what is a fair value that you may expect for it. The word 'fair' is interesting. It describes a group of people coming together to buy and sell. Because there are more buyers, a fair price will reflect market supply and demand so that a 'fair price' is achieved. A fair price may not be exactly the same as an open market price but can be considered to be close enough for our practical purposes.

The legal test for 'every possible purchaser' being involved is one of reasonableness, or has the seller made a reasonable effort to find possible purchasers? If he has, perhaps by advertising widely or employing professional intermediaries to market the company, the price achieved can be considered an open market one.

Why bother to have a valuation?

One approach might be to simply pick a price that represents all the years of work you have put into the business, an amount that you need to retire or possibly the sum of money you want for your next project. After all, you want a decent return and the price is designed to give it to you. If a buyer wants the business, they will just have to pay your asking price. It may be possible to justify your price with a simple valuation working back to the figure you want. The dangers with this method of pricing are, first, that your price may be too high to tempt anyone into making an offer or, second, equally bad, the price you thought up may be too low and leave you selling below the amount you should have achieved.

Prospective purchasers are not interested in the years of work you have put into building the business or how much you need to retire. What they want to buy is the future potential your business will give them together with the assets owned by the company.

Before you can offer your business for sale you need a valuation. Your valuation is your guide to what the business might sell for. It helps you establish what you can realistically expect. Without it, your sales particulars will be incomplete. If there is no indicative price, buyers will not know where to start. As a potential purchaser negotiates the deal, he will form his own valuation and use it to adjust his offer or, if the difference is to great, back out of the purchase. By having done your own valuation at the beginning, you will know that your asking price is realistic. If you have used a similar method to price the company, as your buyer uses, the two valuations will be close and a deal easier to achieve.

Exit Strategy

There are three standard approaches to valuing a business for sale. These are: -

Net asset value.

Comparison with a similar company.

The capitalisation of future income.

Each method of arriving at a valuation is appropriate for different types of company.

The first, net asset value looks at the balance sheet of your company accounts to give a valuation. It is simply the value of the assets in the business less the liabilities expressed in a monetary form. However, company accounts, even when audited, can be misleading. Fixed assets such as premises may be grossly undervalued and need reappraising in line with the current market. Plant and machinery may be overvalued. Computers and software that are still shown as a major asset may be almost worthless. Stock and work in progress may be undervalued to reduce the current tax liability. Debts shown as current assets may not be recoverable and need writing off.

For a net asset valuation to have real use it should be done so that all classes of assets and liabilities are corrected to give a realistic picture of the worth of the business.

A net asset valuation would be appropriate where the business is close to liquidation or there is very little net profit being generated. A company with a large property portfolio and very little revenue would be a candidate for a net asset valuation. There is no goodwill provision in a net asset valuation and it may be possible to achieve a higher capital return by breaking up the company.

You would not normally use a net asset valuation for a thriving trading company with evidence of a steady profit stream.

Another option is comparison with a similar company.

By looking for a similar company that has recently been sold or valued, it is possible to gauge what the market will stand in terms of price. The problem arises when you start to look for the similar company. By their nature, private companies keep their affairs private and, even if you can establish how much one of your competitors was sold for, a comparison is difficult to make. The company that was sold may have a turnover that is similar to your business and it may even make the same types of products. Even so, there will be differences between the businesses, which you do not know about, that make the comparison unreliable. The company you are looking at may be operating with bigger net margins making it more valuable. It may own a large plot of land next to its factory, ripe for development, which had substantially added to the price that the buyer was prepared to pay. The buyer may have been prepared to pay a premium price for the company because it fitted perfectly with his future objectives, something that is unlikely to be repeated.

Because it is difficult to collect the information to make a comparison with a private company, it is tempting to look at a similar publicly quoted business where far more detail is in the public domain. The Shares Valuation Division of the Inland Revenue frequently uses figures from quoted companies to arrive at the value of shares in privately owned companies. The reasons are not difficult to understand when you realise that publicly quoted companies of a similar size have a higher value by virtue of the ease with which their shares can be bought or sold. The Inland Revenue's job is to collect taxes. They know that if they drive up the share valuation of a private company the potential tax liability increases.

Making a comparison between a private and a public company can be misleading and there is no point in comparing companies of different sizes where critical mass and economies of scale will alter fundamentals. While comparisons need to be treated with care understanding what companies are being bought and how much is being paid is knowledge that will help you frame a price for your business. Ask your intermediaries for advice and learn from their experience of recent deals.

Finally there is the capitalisation of future income.

This is the most common technique used to value a private company and the method used by most potential buyers. Businesses that are trading profitably are normally valued using this style of valuation. Using income capitalisation can also be described as 'a discounted cash flow model' or

'Return on Investment'. It is the tool favoured by most potential acquirers.

In order to produce a valuation based on future income, it is necessary to have the trading history of the business, usually going back at least three years. The profits that have been generated during this period are projected forwards to product a forecast of future profit that the business will generate. Part of the valuation process is to discount the future profits to correct for inflation, the cost of the money and the risk of the investment. A ratio is used to convert annual profit to a value for the business. A typical ratio can give a valuation between 4 and 7 times the annual profit. The ratio of profit to value of the business will vary depending on the industry, the state of the market, general economic outlook and other variables within the business.

Fundamentally, the buyer is looking at how long it will take him to get his investment back in relation to any risk. Buying a company where the return on the investment made just matches the bank rate and there is some risk would not worthwhile. It would be simpler and safer for the buyer to put the money in an interest bearing deposit account and watch it grow. Increase the rate of return however with a lower price and the buyer will become more interested. The higher return on investment now on offer makes the business proposition more attractive to the buyer.

One benefit of studying the potential future profit is the chance it gives a buyer to consider if his potential investment in the business is going to give him a high enough rate of return to justify the deal. Without

Exit Strategy

having the right rate of return, it is unlikely that he will go ahead and buy. Part of the buyer's calculations, that the seller will not be told about, are the alterations the buyer makes to the forecasts for changes he intends to introduce to the business after buying it. He may be able to make the business more profitable through economies of scale or moving production elsewhere. These changes can alter the buyer's negotiating position during the sale, particularly if his revised projections turn out lower than the seller's.

Prospective buyers understand that the owner manager of a private company wants to maximise his return and will allow certain adjustments to profit shown in the accounts where a justification can be made. For example if an owner can show that he has been using company funds to entertain lavishly or pay for personal goods, a buyer will add the cost back to the profit figure. If the seller has been paying himself an extremely high wage - a common feature of successful private companies - part of the extra wage can also be added back to the profit figure used to make the projection. Replacing the old owner with a manager paid a realistic salary and stopping the lavish expense account will immediately increase the profitability of the business.

If there have been 'one off' costs such as redundancy payments or the cost of losing an industrial tribunal, these can also be added back to the profit figures. It is unlikely however that a buyer will allow for cash being removed from the business in the past or profits hidden by falsifying stocktaking figures to reduce tax.

Most buyers suspect the seller's figures and tend to assume lower than projected future profits will be generated. A buyer's perspective of what can be added back and what can't will often differ from the seller's. When asked what two plus two equalled, the television mogul Lord Grade replied "Buying or selling?"

What about goodwill?

One aspect of the capitalisation of income calculation is that the valuation produced can be higher than a value obtained by looking at the asset value of the business. The difference between the two valuations is the premium that a buyer is prepared to pay for the future performance of the company and is referred to as 'goodwill'.

Goodwill is intangible. It has no value in itself and the amount of goodwill a buyer is prepared to accept will depend on other aspects of the deal. If there are not enough assets in the business compared to the goodwill, the buyer is likely to reduce his offer or walk away from the deal.

Compare two similar companies for sale. Both produce similar profits but one has a large freehold factory in its asset register together with machinery that is paid for while the second leases a factory and rents all its equipment. Using an income capitalisation valuation would give a similar price for both businesses but the second company is a more risky proposition than the first. The buyer would discount his profit forecast and reduce the price offered accordingly.

Exit Strategy

It follows from this comparison that there is considerable complexity in making a valuation. To add to the confusion the different methods of arriving at a value can become mixed to create a hybrid model trying to correct for the variations found in each business.

However the valuation is made, you should remember that it is only an opinion of what the business might sell for in an open market. It cannot allow for outside influences that might affect the sale such as finding a buyer prepared to pay above the market price or the market collapsing because of an economic recession. Despite this it is still necessary to have a valuation before you start marketing the company.

Graham Watkins

6   *Howdy stranger.*

In the 1998 film The Negotiator Lieutenant Chris Sabian said, 'I am a stranger to you. You have no idea what I am capable of.'

The premises are freshly decorated: there is an exciting buzz in the office and the accounts are looking good. Your exit planning and preparations are complete. It is time to put out the for-sale board and begin your marketing campaign in earnest.

There are a number of different strategies that can be used to offer the business for sale. One obvious way is to advertise the business in suitable trade publications and wait for the enquiries. This shotgun approach can be appropriate for some businesses and is attractive because of its simplicity but it carries some risk.

Your advertisement will need to contain enough information to interest buyers. It will almost certainly have to reveal the business sector you are in together with the size of your company and its profitability.

Even if you withhold the name of the business and ask for enquiries to go to a post office box your competitors - and their staff - will quickly suspect that your business is on the market. While some competitors may be interested in making an offer, others will not and the gossip will begin, damaging the standing and credibility of your company.

It is likely that your employees read the same publications and, seeing the advert, can jump to conclusions particularly when competitors ring up to ask if the rumours are true. Another group that will have their ear close to the ground are your suppliers. People talk and the rumour mill will quickly swing into action. A business that is up for sale is often seen as having something wrong with it, a lame duck to be avoided.

You can avoid this problem is to give very little information about the company in your advertisement. By revealing fewer facts, it becomes more difficult for anyone to guess which business is on the market. Unfortunately, censoring details makes the business bland and less attractive to potential purchasers, achieving exactly the opposite of your objective, of getting possible buyers beating a path to your door.

There are other drawbacks to blind advertising. The potential market is limited to people who read the advert and many that might otherwise be interested may never see it. Even if a potential buyer sees your advert, its size and the limited amount of information given may not be sufficient to grab his interest. Your small general announcement to the world will not have the personal intimacy needed to demand a response from someone who has many other pressing and more interesting issues to deal with.

An alternative and often more suitable way to find prospective buyers is to seek them out in small groups or one at a time. There is no general announcement to the world that a business similar to yours is for sale and the likelihood of rumours starting is reduced.

Instead your agent prepares a buyers' shortlist.

Creating a shortlist of possible purchasers enables you to screen the people who are unlikely to make an offer and also avoids broadcasting to time wasters or the generally inquisitive, leaving you free to concentrate on genuine prospects. Prepare the list correctly and there will be enough potential buyers to make a fair market for your company. It may not be quite an open market but for the purpose of selling a business there is little practical difference between a fair and an open market price. While a possible buyer may be missed, the trade off in terms of managing the sale process makes short-listing a worthwhile option.

But who, you ask, goes on the shortlist?

This is where your selling agent really starts to earn his fees. The first and easiest prospects to include are the ones that you already know in your industry. Competitors, suppliers and even customers are all potential buyers of your company. Although this group is the first to include they are often the last to approach. There are a number of reasons for keeping them in reserve. For one thing the people already in your industry are the most likely group to reveal that your business is for sale either maliciously or by accident. Another issue is the risk that a competitor who has access to your company and its innermost workings will be tempted to steal information, ideas and even key staff instead of buying your company. Usually, it is better to approach this group last, giving them less time to dig around and putting them at a disadvantage to other potential buyers. Bringing competitors in after other possible buyers makes your business appear more attractive and the need for urgency puts them under pressure. Faced with the prospect of a big, aggressive company buying your business and expanding it can quickly focus a competitor's attention resulting in them making a good offer partly to protect their position in the market.

Before you can decide which potential buyers to include on your list, you need to establish some selection criteria. It may be that you want to sell for cash rather than have an exchange of shares or payments made in stages over a period of time. If so, the buyers on your list need to be capable of financing the deal. You may feel moral responsibility for your staff and require that the buyer is not a foreign company that will move production abroad or a competitor who may take over your production and sack your workforce. You may decide that risks to your confidentiality or personal antagonisms make certain companies inappropriate suitors even if they can afford to buy your business.

One potential group of buyers that you may consider approaching are your existing management team. By offering them an opportunity to buy, you are rewarding them for past effort and loyalty. Selling to an existing management team through a management buy out will involve outside financiers and often requires the seller to maintain an involvement in the business for longer than with a simple trade sale. If you prefer to withdraw in stages, a management buy out may be your preferred option and place your managers at the top of the shortlist.

For a quick, clean deal with the best possible price, regardless of future consequences for the business or staff, a trade sale to an outside party is normally the best approach and quality not quantity is the key to building a good buyers shortlist.

At this stage you must keep control.

One important point about the shortlist is that you control it. No sales approaches should be made without your prior approval. This check stops the sale particulars of your company being sent to anyone who your agent does not appreciate is a potential threat. This might include competitors you have not told him about or key customers where the news that your company is up for sale might damage a sensitive negotiation or trading arrangement.

As your agent is building a prospective buyers list, he will be gathering information about your company by asking questions and learning about the business. He uses this information to prepare a company synopsis sometimes referred to as 'initial sales particulars' or 'short sales particulars'. This document is used to generate initial interest in your business.

The synopsis should be short, no more than two or three pages, easy to read, accurate, honest and show the best features of your business. Typical initial sales documents include a brief description of the business, the market in which it operates, products and staffing structure. While the business will not be named, the synopsis will feature turnover and profitability figures, prominently supported by a location and details of premises, but not the address, customer base and type of operation together with reasons for selling (usually retirement since it sounds best) together with a bullet point list of the main features of the business.

The idea is to give enough information to interested prospects so they ask for more and enable indifferent parties to say 'no' quickly. Correctly written, the synopsis will filter out unlikely prospects leaving a small number of potential buyers worth investing more time on.

It's time to make the approach.

The next step is for your agent to begin sending your company synopsis to potential buyers together with an introductory letter addressed to the chief executive or chairman by name and marked 'Private and Confidential'. Your agent follows up the synopsis a couple of days later by telephone and asks to speak to the recipient. Because of the nature of the call, he is usually put through to the right person and is quickly able to establish if there is any interest. The approach letter and follow up phone-calls all originate from the

Exit Strategy

agents office, protecting the identity of your company and avoiding the danger of enquiries being made direct to your company.

Prospects who are not interested are removed from the list and your agent continues on to the next. It is laborious but the size of the transaction justifies the time taken in making these personal approaches. To keep control, the agent will normally send a few approaches at a time, clearing each batch before sending out the next. This manages the amount of interest since your agent can stop if he is inundated with enquiries for more information. Before more information is given to any interested parties your agent will ask them to sign a confidentiality agreement.

It's that word again, confidentiality and it's as important as ever.

A confidentiality agreement is a strongly worded legal document that makes plain your requirement that the interested party undertakes to abide by certain conditions before being given any more information about your business. By signing and returning the agreement, the buyer accepts your conditions of confidentiality and these can, in theory, be enforced with legal redress if the undertakings are broken. The buyer promises to keep confidential any information subsequently given about your business and to keep confidential the fact that negotiations to buy your company are being entered into. Other clauses usually included in the confidentiality document are an undertaking to make no direct approaches but to deal only through the selling and a condition prohibiting the buyer from offering any of your employees a job for a specified period. This undertaking is designed to make it difficult to poach key staff.

Such forceful undertakings are necessary because your buyer and his advisors will be given all the secrets that enable your business to operate competitively. Sensitive information such as supplier relationships, buying prices, margins and details of your key customers' discounts will all be revealed. If these secrets were taken and used by a competitor, significant damage might be done to your business. As well as learning about your trading relationships, the potential buyer will discover who your key employees are and their remuneration. The temptation to steal them away with a better offer is understandable.

A large company considering buying your business will normally understand and respect your need for confidentiality. Difficulties are generally caused by smaller and less experienced buyers or competitors looking at your business. Are they considering making an offer or are they fishing for ideas and staff to use in their own operation?

It would be foolhardy for any seller to disclose any information or allow outsiders access to the innermost secrets of a company without obtaining a legally enforceable confidentiality agreement beforehand. In practice, it can sometimes be difficult to enforce an agreement where a potential buyer has broken a confidence but insisting on the agreement is still valuable since it makes clear that you regard the issue of secrecy as very important.

Exit Strategy

Now it's time to reveal your detailed business profile.

Once your potential buyers have signed and returned the confidentiality agreement, they will require a lot more information about your business. They will want a detailed business profile and your agent should have this document ready to be issued. The detailed profile of your company is the document that the buyer studies as part of his preliminary investigation into your company. It needs to be comprehensive enough to enable the buyer to make a conditional offer. This is a key-selling document designed to promote your business to its best advantage.

A detailed business profile might include the following sections. I've included eleven but the number and headings may vary: -

First an Executive summary.

The summary includes an introduction to the business, its location, products and markets together with some details of customer profiles and marketing strategies. As a selling document, it highlights the principle attractions of the business and gives some financial information; usually turnover, adjusted profit figures for the last few years and some balance sheet information. The summary also details who owns the business and the reasons for the sale.

Secondly a Brief history.

By explaining the history of the business, the profile builds substance to the offer. Detailing how long the company has traded together with the dates of significant changes add to the perception of a business moving forward and suggests that the business has momentum and growth potential. A business that is moving forwards is worth more than one that is standing still or stagnating. Accolades such as achieving 'Investors in People' status and other advances can be flagged up, demonstrating the dynamic character of the business.

Thirdly Nature of operations.

This section describes the nature of the operation and contains different sections breaking the business down into its constituent parts. These can include how the business does its marketing, sales, the manufacturing process, special projects, website usage and other areas that are relevant to explain the success of the company.

Fourthly information about customers and competition.

Talking about customers and competitors demonstrates that your business is aware of its position in the market. Strengths such as a large and diverse customer base or strong key account relationships are highlighted to demonstrate stability and growth potential. Reference to competitor activity illustrates awareness and confidence in the operation.

Fifthly some Supplier details.

Exit Strategy

Continuity of supply is a significant issue for a buyer. The potential buyer wants to know that there is more than one source for key materials and products or that the buying position of the business has been secured by contracts with your suppliers. Supply chain details can include brief terms of trade and explain how prices are subject to renegotiation.

Sixth property details.

Property owned or leased by the business is explained in the detailed business profile. If there is a substantial property owned by the business, the buyer may need to use it as collateral to fund the purchase of the business. If the premises are leased, a buyer may want to know that there is a lengthy term left on the lease. By having a long lease he can be confident that there will be no disruptions cause by a forced move of the business. However if the buyer intends to close the operation down and move it elsewhere he may prefer a short lease that is less expensive to break.

Seventh an explanation of you management organisation and control.

The buyer will want to understand the management organization, will need to be assured the business will operate smoothly after the takeover and will be looking closely at the management. This section also outlines how the accounts are done, what accounting and other software is used, if the software is standard or bespoke and how the systems are supported. How customer records are stored, how credit is controlled, how the website is administered, who deals with the payroll and the staff structure of the business are all questions that can be answered here. Charts illustrating the organisational structure and other areas can be included as appendix items to this information.

Eighth some trading information.

The trading information relates to the financial performance of the business over the last four or five years and is an abridged form of the audited profit and loss accounts, together with explanatory notes.

Ninth a current balance sheet.

This section includes the balance sheet complementing the trading information given above together with notes explaining any unusual items like exceptional stock levels or an unusual level of debtors.

Tenth notes on the business profile.

This is where your advisor will cover his back with the usual disclaimers - All information in this business profile has been provided by the directors. Any purchaser should make his own enquiries and take appropriate independent advice before investing. Realistically it would be naive for any seller to be dishonest about the details of the business or its performance since any material distortions would quickly be revealed when the buyer's advisors start checking everything.

Finally eleventh an appendix.

Exit Strategy

The appendix contains supporting paperwork including organisational charts, corporate brochures and product literature together with a copy of the most recent audited accounts.

Including so much information in the detailed business profile makes it a substantial document that requires careful preparation and thorough checking before it is issued to any prospective purchaser.

Some potential buyers will study the profile and withdraw, explaining to your agent that they are no longer interested. Your business may not fit with their existing operation or acquiring your company might not suit their overall strategy. Once a buyer withdraws, your agent moves on remembering to ask for the safe return of the business profile. It is still your property and remains a confidential document.

Now it's time to prepare your business for some unusual visitors.

Buyers, who are still interested after studying your business profile, will have further questions and will, almost certainly, need to visit your company. They want to see for themselves how the business operates. Your agent will arrange the details of each visit and agree a cover story with the buyer so that the group, or groups, of people arriving to look around, do not unsettle staff. You might explain the visitors as potential customers, suppliers or even a party from the Chamber of Commerce. Before the visit, encourage your employees to look smart and efficient as the visitors walk around. They need motivating to feel enthusiastic and look proud of where they work.

The subterfuge may feel distasteful but it is important. To create the right impression you need the business to buzz as the visitors walk around. Your employees are on offer as part of the business and you want them to look their best. Before the visit, your agent should ask the buyer's team to make sure that no confidential questions or sensitive issues are raised in front of your staff.

Part of your preparation is to learn about the prospective buyer. Learning about his existing business and exploring why he is interested in your company will help you understand what he may think are important positive areas of your business. Effort spent understanding your buyer and his motives beforehand will make it easier to conduct the visit. The buyer already knows a great deal about your business and learning about his will make the meeting less one sided. Get your agent to ask the buyer if there are any specific areas he wants to see or discuss during the visit.

The scene is now set for the next stage of the sale. The buyer arrives together with advisors and possibly his financial backers. Your agent accompanies the buyer's team, observing their reactions and comments as you show them around. Apparently casual comments from the buyer's party can reveal potential strengths of your offer or show up problems that need addressing for the sale to go through successfully. His observations during the visit are important and helpful during the negotiations to come.

Exit Strategy

Part of the visit can include a private discussion giving the buyer and his team an opportunity to ask confidential questions about your company. As the visit comes to an end, ask for any further queries to be raised through your agent.

A buyer that is enthusiastic about making an offer will contact your agent shortly after the company visit and either make an offer or ask for a further meeting to discuss terms. More cagey buyers will sit and wait until your agent telephones to enquire if the buyer is satisfied with what he saw and considering making an offer to buy your business.

Graham Watkins

7   *Let's deal.*

You don't get what you deserve; you get what you negotiate.

During the sale of my business, my agent stopped me as we were going into a crucial meeting where we hoped to do the deal and said, 'Graham, you don't get what you deserve. You get what you negotiate.' He then went on to tell me how we should conduct the meeting. We had already planned our strategy but his advice was sound and it was a lesson well learned. Let me explain.

A potential buyer now has enough information and is interested in buying your company. He may have made an offer already through your agent and it's time to get the offer improved. The moment has arrived to negotiate the deal and the best way to negotiate is face to face. A meeting is needed so that you can strike a bargain and begin to sell your business. But this is no ordinary sales presentation. It may be the biggest and most complex sale you will ever make. Go into this meeting poorly prepared, intending to rely on your selling and negotiating skills or natural charm and you will come away disappointed. You may still do a deal but will it have been the best that you might have achieved?

Firstly preparation is essential.

A good salesman will prepare for a sales presentation. He will know his product inside out, all its features and benefits, weaknesses and unique points. He will be confident that what he is selling is extra special. Part of his enthusiasm comes from this confidence. The same must apply to selling a business. You - and your agent - must understand the business and project its strengths with confidence. This won't be hard since you have promoted your company many times before, to staff, customers, the bank and other interested audiences. Because you have been running your business, you know how it works and if you have been grooming the business to sell, your enthusiasm will already be focused. But knowledge of the business is not enough.

Professional salesmen don't only study their product. They learn about the marketplace. Your agent's experience can help here. He can advise you about current trends, how well businesses are selling, the eagerness of funders to lend and the prices being achieved for comparable companies. You need to understand this background information so that you can conduct your negotiation. Without this knowledge you can have no idea if an offer is a good one or not. You will be dealing in the dark.

You also need to know your buyer. The person you will be negotiating with? Can you empathise with him as a negotiating equal? What about his organisation? How big is it? Why are they interested in making the deal? What areas of your business are they particularly attracted to and what bits might present problems? How will your business fit their operation and will it add value to the rest of their business?

Until now, your agents will have been the main contact with the buyer. He will have had correspondence and phone conversations and been present during their visits to your premises. Your agent will have developed an understanding of the buyer's motivation and position. Ask him for his views and do more research to build your own picture of the buying side. Look at their accounts, product literature, press releases, their history of buying companies and any other information available that will give you an insight into their business strategy. Understanding a buyer's motivation and strategy improves your negotiating position.

Your opponent will appreciate the maxim 'knowledge is power' and will be looking at you and your business in the same way but he has one big advantage. You have already sent him a lot of detailed information about your business.

Decide who will lead the negotiation from your side. If you feel uncomfortable negotiating or are not sure that you can stay calm under pressure, let your agent do the talking while you sit back listening and observing. If you are really nervous you may even prefer not to go to the negotiation, leaving the whole thing to your agent. Generally though, this is a mistake since, if a question was asked, for example, about the business that the agent cannot answer, your absence could stop the negotiation. The same thing would happen if an offer was made that needed you approval. You need to be there to deal with issues as well as motivate and enthuse your side.

Secondly establish your objectives before you start.

Before the negotiation meeting, you need to sit down with your agent and agree what you want to achieve. The most obvious objective is a good price but what does that mean? You will have valued the business as part of your early preparation and know what realistic price you can expect. Talk through the options with your agent and agree what your lowest price or bottom price will be. This is the price below which you walk away from the deal. Above your bottom price will be the fair price you can realistically expect and, above that, the price you dream of achieving. Perhaps this will be your starting price at the negotiating table.

Getting a good price will not be your only objective. How long are you prepared to wait for your money? Do you want to get paid in cash and leave the business immediately or are you prepared to take a part payment and wait for the balance to be paid, in instalments, over several years? Are you prepared to compromise by waiting and achieving a higher price in return? Is the trade off worth the risk? What is your position if the offer is for an exchange of shares instead of cash? Understanding the buyer's likely strategy will help you work out possible negotiating positions.

Exit Strategy

Suppose the buyer offers to buy some of the shares now and the remainder later on at a valuation to be made at that time. Such a deal involves a risk that the new owner runs the business down and you get a lower price for the future share transaction. Conversely the value may go up. Work out a strategy with your agent for dealing with such an offer before the meeting. Don't wait to be surprised. Are you willing to give non-competitive undertakings or do you intend to start again the next day in a similar business? How long are you prepared to continue working in the business and on what terms? You need to work out preferred and a fall-back position for each issue and rank them in importance, ready to sacrifice some during the negotiation.

A key worry for potential buyers is the possibility that you are selling up because of some imminent problem they do not know about. To protect themselves from this risk buyers sometimes try to tie the price to future profitability. By linking the two, the buyer is reducing his risk and making you gamble on the business continuing to perform well. This sort of arrangement, known as 'earn-out' or 'contingency payments' may be appropriate if you are staying on to help run the business. If an 'earn-out' is acceptable - and it may be if you feel bullish about future performance - you need to establish your negotiating position in advance. How long do you want the earn-out to last? Do you want to be paid partly as a bonus for the remaining shares? Understand the tax implications for both sides and what works best for you.

What contingent risks are you prepared to accept to protect the buyer's future exposure? Most buyers will be looking for you to indemnify them against undeclared liabilities. If there are any awkward issues that can undo the deal or weaken your position, you want them out in the open before the negotiating meeting. Don't spring nasty surprises on a buyer as you are negotiating price. He won't like it.

By listing objectives and mapping out your meeting strategy you significantly increase your chances of concluding a successful negotiation, one where you achieve what you want. Without these objectives you have no way of measuring the deal to know if it is a good one.

Thirdly plan to build in flexibility.

While you have been preparing for the meeting, your buyer and his advisors will have been doing the same. If there is a large gap in the expectations or objectives of the two sides, the meeting will be a difficult one and a deal less likely. To stand a better chance of succeeding, your objectives need to be realistic and to have some flexibility. You will need to win concessions from the buyer and must be prepared to give some in return. Negotiating is a game where players trade off or compromise on differences between their starting positions. Some of your positions, your bottom price for example, will not be negotiable so you will need to have other stances that can be traded in return for movement from the buyer. Planning in flexibility gives you the option of letting your buyer win points during the negotiation while you quietly achieve your principle objectives. In a good negotiation, even one that is bruising at times, everyone leaves satisfied that they have won something.

A bargain made after a good negotiation is more likely to get completed than one where the meeting has been dominated by one strong side. When this occurs the weaker side reflects and realises how inadequately they prepared for the negotiation. They know it's a bad deal for them and back out wasting everyone's time and effort, a situation that could have been avoided with the right preparation.

A word about the venue.

'Your place or mine?' is not the right question when arranging a negotiating meeting. By convention, negotiating the deal is done on neutral ground and there are good reasons for this. The negotiations can be lengthy and complex. Meeting in a conference facility or hotel allows everyone to concentrate on the negotiating. There are no phones or staff with urgent messages to disrupt or cause minds to wander.

How many people attend the negotiation is also a factor. The buyer might bring two other directors, his advisor/agent, an accountant and a financial backer. Seven people and that is just one side of the negotiating table. Conducting such a large and important meeting within your business can be disruptive and impractical. The meeting may be confidential but curious staff will soon speculate about why so many people are in the building. Another benefit of selecting a neutral location is that neither side has an advantage because they are playing at home.

The venue needs to be large enough, comfortable and with seating that allows the participants to take part as equals. Sitting around a boardroom table is a good option. Refreshments should be available and adequate time allocated by all sides to complete the negotiations. Strangely, custom is that the seller usually picks up the bill for the meeting room.

Let's talk now about what you should do during the negotiation.

It is a good strategy to take control of the meeting from the start. You can do this by beginning the discussion with a short history of contact so far and stating the objectives of today's meeting. By describing the reason for the meeting, simply and in mutually beneficial terms, you begin to build forward momentum. Both sides understand why they are there and the brief history is a reminder that everyone has already invested time in the process. Today's negotiation is the next logical step.

Use the 'we' word.

Use the 'we' word to emphasise that both sides are working towards the same outcome. Say that you are confident that 'we' can strike a deal and ask the other-side for their view. Listen carefully to their response and make sure you understand what is being said.

List the issues.

The next stage is to draw out, in neutral terms, the points that need to be discussed. While making the

Exit Strategy

list, do not discuss any of the topics. Begin by asking the buyer what issues he has. The buyer may start by saying you need to negotiate a price and immediately offer an amount. It would be tempting to react and start a discussion about what the price should be but discussing price at this stage is a mistake. Trying to deal with price, usually one of the most difficult issues, before other peripheral subjects have been agreed would be like negotiating the price of a car before agreeing its specification and how many accessories are included.

Another problem with starting to negotiate before you have established what all the issues are and agreeing an agenda is that you have given control of the meeting to the buyer. He can now introduce obstacles in any order and flit confusingly from subject to subject. Confusion during the negotiation makes it difficult to marshal your arguments and gives the buyer an advantage.

Instead of reacting, simply agree that the price needs discussing and add it to the list of issues. Remain calm but don't forget to make a mental note of the amount offered, remembering it may be useful later.

Remain neutral while you list the negotiating points and add any topics that you have, again, in mutually positive terms. If the buyer is aggressive or raises something that surprises you, do not react. Listen carefully to what the buyer is saying and stay cool.

When you believe the list is complete make sure by asking the buying side if there are any other points that need to be added. The assorted collection of negotiating points now needs to be turned into an agenda.

While this process has been described as happening during one meeting, it is quite possible that the agents have collected the issues together beforehand and prepared an agenda. If they have, so much the better since you then have more time to prepare for each point the buyer has raised.

The running order for the agenda needs careful consideration. The first item needs to be one that can be easily and quickly settled. Getting agreement on a point quickly maintains forward momentum and creates a positive negotiating atmosphere, one where 'we' can do this deal. The two sides are beginning to move together.

Starting with a hot, difficult issue begins the negotiation badly. It is too soon, neither side has settled down and an early confrontation makes it more difficult to continue in a positive way. Positions quickly become entrenched making even easy differences harder to agree. It is better to keep more contentious points back and deal with them later on when both sides have become more comfortable and are inclined to work harder for a solution.

Arrange the agenda to start with the easiest issue and end with the thorniest gives the negotiating relationship time to strengthen before you have to deal with the awkward subjects and the time everyone has already invested in the meeting acts to encourage conciliation towards the end, when it is needed the most.

Exit Strategy

Strategically speaking, leaving the most difficult items until the end makes it sensible to be prepared to give concessions early and seek their return later on.

A good strategy is to refine the issues.

You are now getting into the body of the negotiation. Take each issue in turn and discuss it. If it is a buyer's agenda item, ask him to start and explain exactly what he wants. Does his request meet the position you planned to accept? If it does, that's great. You can cross another item of the list and are another small step closer to selling your business. How you cross it off the list is up to you. You may simply agree the point with the buyer or if you want to play hard you may argue before finally telling the buyer that what he is asking is costing you dearly as you concede. You may, however, realise that you cannot accept the position as it is proposed and need to change it. Refining the issue is one way to change its nuance to your advantage. For example, your buyer may ask you for an undertaking to stay out of the industry for three years. He sees you as a threat and wants this promise from you to protect his investment in your company. Refining the issue to include certain geographic regions may satisfy him and leave you an opportunity to start up again. Your buyer may not agree to this proposal leaving you with the choice of accepting his position, rejecting it out of hand or agreeing but asking for a concession in return.

As part of your strategy you should make sure that there are few points that are just given to the other side. Even where the issue is minor, one that costs you nothing to give away, you should still seek a concession in return. That may seem pointless but to simply give in moves the dynamic towards the buyer. By allowing the buyer to dictate terms you will lose the initiative and strengthen the buyer's position. This does not mean that you should risk breaking the deal on minor issues and it is quite reasonable to ask for concessions that have little value to the buyer or yourself. The important point is to continue to negotiate as equals.

Refining issues involves discussion, giving and taking, defending and attacking until a bargain has been reached on each point. Normally it is better to settle each issue before moving on and, if the agenda has been programmed in the right order, the movement from one settled item to the next becomes logical and simple.

Occasionally, a matter that looks quite easy to resolve becomes a real obstacle and might even break the deal. Both sides dig in and no trade off or compromise can be found. When that happens propose, that the unresolved point is put on one side and dealt with as the last item at the end of the meeting. This allows both sides to back off and reflect on their position without losing face. Towards the end of the negotiations all parties begin to focus on closing the deal. This motivates both sides towards finding a solution and a compromise is usually quickly found for the obstruction.

But there will be times when you need to fall back.

During the negotiation, the buyer and the seller will be moving from their best stance on each issue to their fall-back position. If the negotiation starts with the sides close together the outcome will be quickly reached. However, where they are further apart, far more negotiation is needed for the deal to happen.

Use trial balloons to test the buyer's willingness to move his position. Ask 'What if we…?' to make a proposal without committing yourself. By using the 'we' word you are suggesting co-operation. You and the buyer are trying to find a way forward together while at the same time you are gently probing his position. Don't worry if the buyer dismisses your trial balloon. You can always send up another one.

If all else fails, ask the buyer for help. Tell him he is expecting too much from you and that you cannot see a way around the issue. This warns the buyer that you are close to your fallback position and have nowhere to go. His response may well be to soften his demand or help you by suggesting a suitable trade-off enabling you to agree.

As you concede or compromise an issue, explain how expensive the concession is to you. Making the other side realise they are asking a lot from you helps your next position sound more reasonable. After each point is agreed, summarise how it was resolved. Repeating back to the buyer what has been decided helps clarify progress and avoids disputes later on. It also gives you another opportunity to slightly refine what was agreed to your advantage. Make notes confirming exactly what was settled.

While this is all happening don't forget to communicate with your agent.

During your negotiation there will be times when you need to think about an issue or discuss its ramifications with your advisors. You may feel overwhelmed by the buyer's attacking posture or unsure of a technical term used. Suggest that the meeting is adjourned for a few minutes and leave, taking your team somewhere private. It is quite reasonable to tell the buyer that you want to take advice on a point or that you just need a break. Sitting down outside the meeting gives an opportunity to compare notes with your advisors, to take stock and devise new stratagems if they are needed. Breaks are important chances for your team to communicate privately and observations by the rest of your team can reveal ways forward that the lead negotiator has missed.

Sometimes a buyer will ambush you. Be prepared for some nasty surprises.

You may think every point to be discussed is on the agenda when a buyer suddenly adds a surprise demand. Calling for a break is a useful ploy if this happens. It gives you time to think and discuss the surprise question with your team before you respond. Point out that the issue is not on the agenda and ask if the buyer has any others that he wants to add as you call for the break. Doing so, signals that you don't expect to negotiate in this way. Consider the surprise issue and how it affects matters already agreed. If it does, you can reasonably go back and renegotiate them pointing out that the extra question the buyer raised changes your position.

Exit Strategy

As you negotiate don't forget to add value with concessions.

Ideally, negotiations include winning concessions that are worth more to you than your opponent while your opponent wins concessions that have value to him but cost you little. Say the buyer wants an undertaking from you to stay out of the industry for three years. You have already decided that you are retiring, so to agree costs you nothing but for the buyer, such an undertaking has significant value; it protects his investment from competition. During the negotiation you may ask for a higher price than the one on offer. Your prospective buyer counters, offering to pay an extra amount spread over three years. You have won because you have got the higher price that you wanted. At the same time your buyer is able to finance the difference from profit generated within the business and has no extra cash to find. The buyer has worked around the problem that he has no more funds available. Although there is a cost to him, it is deferred and manageable. This sort of flexibility and ingenuity helps both sides win.

Finally, don't overplay your position it could cost you the sale.

If you feel that you are on a winning streak and your buyer is giving in easily, you may be tempted to push harder and win an even better deal. Be careful! There is a risk associated with over negotiating your position. Although your buyer appears to be a pushover, he may be close to his bottom line and ready to walk away from the table. By negotiating hard you can destroy what is already a good deal, leaving you with nothing when the buyer decides he has had enough. It is better to arrive at your planned objective on a position and stop before any damage is done. By the same token, you should never threaten to walk away from the negotiating table over an issue if you do not mean it. The buyer may call your bluff.

Towards the end of the meeting, as the last gaps between the parties are settled, an atmosphere of excitement and relief begins to appear with both sides aware that the deal is nearly done. When the last obstacle is settled you may think the negotiating is over. Sorry, but as you are about to learn this is just the beginning. What you have just negotiated is an agreement to carry on negotiating.

Next comes a Heads of Agreement (Letter of Intent).

After the meeting, your agent produces a document known as 'Heads of Agreement' or 'Letter of Intent'. The purpose of the heads of agreement is to confirm the structure of the deal negotiated including the price and terms for the transaction. However, it is not a binding contract for the sale of your business. The buyer or seller can still back out if they wish.

As well as outlining the contracts structure, the heads of agreement confirms how other details of the transaction are to be settled. It will set out how the final price may vary depending on valuations of premises, stock and work in progress. It may settle how the price varies because of additional profits or losses made by the business up to the time of the final contract. It will confirm how and when the money, referred to as 'the consideration', is paid.

Exit Strategy

Details of the other points settled during the negotiation meeting are also confirmed in the heads of agreement. Some areas will sound rather vague. 'The vendor will provide warranties and indemnities as are appropriate for a transaction of this nature' for example indicates there is more negotiating to come.

Although either side can undo the deal, there are parts of the heads of agreement that are, once the document is signed, legally binding. Normally, the seller will undertake to the buyer that for a set period (maybe 3 or 6 months) the seller will not negotiate with any other potential buyer and will end all negotiations with other parties that have already started. This allows the buyer time to complete further research into the business, known as 'Due Diligence', and prepare the detailed contract for the purchase of the company. So far, the buyer has worked with the information you have supplied. To proceed further he needs to spend time and a considerable amount of money examining the business in more detail. You're agreement not to negotiate with other parties protects the buyer's position and allows him time to complete the deal.

The letter of intent usually confirms that each side will pay its own professional costs and undertakes to maintain confidentiality, except to professional advisors, about the proposed transaction. You may have thought that you had negotiated the sale of your business but it's not over yet. The transaction is about to get a lot more complicated.

Graham Watkins

8   *Here comes the posse.*

Now it's time for the bean counters take over and my chance to repeat a favourite quote. 'Auditors are the crack troops who watch a battle from the safety of a hillside and, when the battle is over, come down to count the dead and bayonet the wounded.'

Once a deal has been agreed in principle, your buyer's auditors and lawyers will start appearing. Their job is to add the detail to what has already been negotiated and to protect the buyer's position. This is done first to test the truthfulness and accuracy of the information that your have supplied and, second, to search the business thoroughly for everything else that the buyer needs to know before he buys your company.

The process is called Due Diligence.

The name given to searching a business before buying. The expression 'Due Diligence' first appeared in 1933 when American legislators described it as a technique employed to obtain 'full and fair disclosure' of facts about public securities, allowing investors to make objective trading decisions. Since then the definition 'Due Diligence' has expanded to describe the process applied by a buyer of a business before he completes the purchase.

Due diligence enables the buyer to look closely at the fundamental elements that drive your business and search for potential risks that may affect its future performance or damage profits. This will include internal issues such as inadequate or obsolete production machinery and external threats like changing market demand or new government regulation. As well as scanning the horizon for future risks, the buyer will look back; searching for anything that has already happened that might damage the business. Examples might be outstanding litigation with a supplier, undeclared tax liabilities or a product warranty dispute.

During due diligence, you are asked to reveal everything that is pertinent about your company. Making a 'full and fair disclosure' is important because you will be required to indemnify the buyer against any loss arising as a result of something you do not disclose. Brushing a problem under the carpet and hoping the buyer does not discover it until after he has paid is not a good idea. The advantage of disclosing everything is that once a problem has been disclosed the buyer cannot use it to complain or seek compensation after the sale has been finalised.

The importance of disclosure makes it necessary for the buyer to conduct the due diligence exercise carefully and in a prescribed manner, one where questions and answers are documented and records of disclosure kept by both sides. This avoids disputes and arguments arising, over exactly what was disclosed. Say, for example, your factory stands on contaminated land. You tell the buyer but no record of the conversation is made. Later, after the sale, the buyer claims that he has only just discovered the contamination and demands that you pay for the site to be cleaned up. If you are unable to prove that you disclosed the contamination, the indemnity you have given can result in a hefty bill that you did not expect. If the disclosure of contamination had been recorded and proven, you would have no liability. The buyer knew about the condition of the land before he finalised the deal making it his problem to clean the site up.

It's essential to use your lawyer to disclose everything.

Getting disclosure right is critical and answering questions asked by the buyer's advisors should be done formally and only through your lawyer. The first step will be for your lawyer to receive a written 'Due diligence request' from the buyer's legal team, which your lawyer will forward to you. Your job is to answer the questions and return the questionnaire to your lawyer together with any supporting documents needed. As well as the due diligence paperwork, you will shortly be receiving a 'Share Acquisition Agreement' from your lawyer. These lengthy and complex documents will be travelling backwards and forwards several times as alterations are made and additional clauses added. Modern email and computer programmes that track document changes make it far easier to handle the intricate paperwork that you are going to have to deal with.

Prepare yourself for a shock before you look at the due diligence request your lawyer sends. A questionnaire for a modest company can extend to 25 pages and contain questions and requests for paperwork explaining 160 different aspects of the business. Few of the questions will be simple requiring yes or no answers and most answers will need several pages of supporting material. Nothing that you have previously experienced during your business career is likely to have prepared you for the barrage of questions that engulf you. This is a fishing expedition for information but there is no finesse of fly or fishing rod. Your business is about to be visited by a deep-sea trawler. You are obliged to answer all the enquiries and supply any documents that are asked for by the buyer. Before long, you will begin to wonder if selling your business is really a good idea.

Here's a very important piece of advice, keep copies of everything.

During the buyer's investigations, some documents will be asked for several times. Your lawyer will need copies to send back with your answers. The buyer's accountants, his lender's accountants and other advisors employed can also ask for the same documents. To make life easier, it is a good idea, right from the start, to keep a copy of every piece of paper you have provided, suitable catalogued in a folder. A lever arch or box file gives easy access and saves you having to search out the original piece of paper every time it is asked for. Originals need to stay in their normal places so the business can continue to use them as required both while you are there and after you have left. Filing your own copies, together with a copy of the due diligence request, gives you a useful record that you might decide to keep after you have left the business. If there is a dispute later, your retained copies can be useful, particularly if the new owner is reluctant, for some reason, to look for the originals once he is in control of the business.

Now you can expect the questions to come thick and fast. 'Tell us about?' will be the cry.

Due diligence investigates all aspects of a company and might typically include questions on the following: -

The company
Asking for the full name of the business, registration details, shareholder details, details of parent or subsidiary companies together with copies of the memorandum and articles of association, details about the statutory books, their upkeep and any shareholder agreements.

Accounts

Asks for details of accounting periods, for copies of audited accounts for the last three years and management accounting records.

Finance
Requires details about all borrowing, loans, equipment finance, guarantees, charges and grants obtained by the business together with supporting documentation.

Trading
Looks at contracts above a certain value or with unusual terms, details of licensing and agency agreements, changes that have taken place in the business in the last year, details of key suppliers and customers, credit terms offered to customers and details of imported or exported goods all with supporting evidence.

Directors and officers
Asks for director's details, remuneration, directors' loans, key-man insurance and for copies of contracts of employment.

Employees
Requires a list of employees, their personal details, remuneration, details of staff turnover during the last three years, bonus schemes, union representation, details of pay review procedure, disabled staff, any disciplinary matters, copies of contracts of employment and company staff handbook.

Claims against the company

Exit Strategy

Asks about disputes with staff that have left in the last three years, any criminal activity where a prosecution is pending or in progress and any health and safety claims.

Pensions
Investigates company pension schemes for directors and staff, sick pay and contingent liabilities.

Assets
Asks for details of vehicles owned by the company, a full inventory of plant and machinery, assets acquired or disposed of during the last three years, details of all mortgages or charges against assets and a breakdown of slow moving or redundant stock.

Computers and IT.
Enquires about bespoke software, standard software and licensing details, hardware together with maintenance and software support details.

Intellectual property
Looks at patents and trademarks with proof of registrations, copyright, licensing agreements, websites, domain registration and hosting details.

Properties
Requires a schedule of properties owned or used by the company together with plans, leases, registered titles, charges and mortgages, planning consents, alterations, disputes and any reports made during the last three years.

Environmental

Asks about any pollution incidents or land contamination, chemicals used on the premises now and by previous users.

Health and safety
Requires a copy of the company's health and safety policy, evidence of COSHH compliance and details of any reportable accidents or claims over the last five years.

Guarantees and security
Asks for details of any guarantees or sureties, indemnities or charges given in favour of the company.

Regulatory
Requires a list and details of any regulatory of licensing authorities with which the company is required to comply.

Insurance
Looks for insurance details and claim history together with any defective product claims, court judgments or possible disputes.

Shareholders
Requests information about the shareholders including details of any criminal record.

Taxation
Examines the tax affairs of the business for the last five years including questions on VAT, corporation tax, PAYE, national insurance contributions, any tax investigations, audits and copies of any agreements made with the tax authorities.

Completing such a detailed questionnaire takes time and you will be thankful once your replies, together with supporting paperwork asked for as evidence, have been sent to the buyer's advisors. Unfortunately, your answers will trigger a further round of enquiries as each answer is dissected and considered. Some of the questions can seem trivial and even impertinent but you should deal with them honestly and calmly. Refusing to answer or being evasive would suggest to the buyer that you have something to hide and prompt further probing.

By now the importance of preparing your company so that it is ready to be sold, explained in chapter three, will have become clear. Without the advance groundwork your answers to due diligence questions will reveal problems that a buyer will not like. Faced with increased risks or uncertainty, your buyer may take fright and walk away from the deal or hit you with a lower offer. Wrong answers revealed during due diligence give the buyer a good renegotiating tool.

And it get worse. The auditors ride again.

The due diligence request is the legal element of disclosure, handled through the lawyers, but it is not the whole story. Your buyer will also instruct his accountants to carry out a full financial study of your company. They will be looking back at audited and management accounts as well as forwards at your projections and forecasts. In addition to examining your accounts, the auditors will be investigating other areas of the business.

Some of the auditors' work can be done away from your offices but aspects of their enquiries will, by necessity, be done at your premises. For example, they may want to examine your accounting software to see how it is set up to produce management accounts or how it links with your customer database. Some of the auditors' investigations can be done in normal operating hours, when employees are present. Others may require a visit when your workforce is not about. For example, they might ask for a demonstration of how your computer network shuts down and recovers using backup data. Such an exercise would not normally be done while dealing with customers and having active computer records in use by staff.

Depending on how vigorous the investigations are, you can find that a team of accountants arrives at your premises and stays for several days during which they badger you continuously for documents and answers to questions. Another party to the transaction who may wish to send an audit team is the funding provider. The financial backer will also need to satisfy himself that your business is worth buying. Fortunately, the buyer and finance provider have similar concerns and usually rely on one firm of accountants to do the study.

There is a danger here. Beware the culture clash.

Accountants are by nature conservative and prone to realism, a characteristic sometimes mistakes for pessimism by entrepreneurs. When it comes to auditing a business, an auditor will report accordingly

Exit Strategy

and his risk aversion makes it is easier to say 'it's a good deal' only after suitable caveats are added. His job is to protect the buyer from unforeseen threats. He will be sceptical and likely to challenge information you have already provided. His responsibility during the due diligence and the difference in culture that exists between accountants and risk taking entrepreneurs can combine to create extra stress during the investigations. If this happens and you feel under pressure during the accountant's visits take a deep breath and keep calm. Nothing will be achieved by arguing with your visitor. He is only doing his job and will be gone soon enough.

Auditors will sometimes justify their fees, to the buyer, by unearthing something the buyer can use to negotiate a lower price. Their remit can be wide and the temptation exists to generally ferret about looking for problems. There is not a lot that you can do about this but, if it happens, remain civil and 'helpful' while being aware that the accountant is not working for your benefit. His job is to report back to the buyer with what he finds.

While the accountants are conducting their investigations they may ask you to confirm points in writing or guarantee that some piece of information is correct. If they do, refuse politely and point out that any written undertakings or guarantees the buyer requires will be dealt with through your lawyers.

While the accountants are on your premises, they must observe the confidentiality agreed by the buyer in the heads of terms. Do not allow the auditors direct access to your staff without prior permission from yourself. If an auditor expresses the wish to interview your employees, only allow him once you have a clear understanding of the purpose of the interviews and are satisfied that they will not compromise your confidentiality. Auditors can observe the business but they should not discuss issues with staff or ask for opinions or comment.

Who else, you ask, might turn up?

Depending on the details of your business, the buyer may feel the need to instruct other advisers to examine your company. These might include specialists in insurance, computers, production, property valuations, marketing or environmental issues or any other area where specialist comment is needed.

It is fair?

For the seller, responding to due diligence is a tedious exercise and often the worst stage of selling a business. As you plough through the questions, keep yourself focused by thinking of the prize at the end. When you creep back to the photocopier, late at night, to print yet another 100 pages, consider that you are also doing this to help the buyer. Your answers are giving the buyer the knowledge he needs to take over and manage your business in just a few weeks, knowledge that has taken you years to accumulate. While the work the due diligence is causing you may seem an injustice, think of your buyer. He is at the start of a learning curve that is positively meteoric.

9   *Meanwhile back at the ranch.*

The Pulitzer Prize winner Norman Mailer wrote, 'What I fear far more than selling out is wearing out.' He also wrote, 'Don't take life to seriously. You won't come out of it alive.' But ,while you are selling the company and getting out, in business life has to go on and that can be a problem.

For the owner who is running his company, selling the business is a major disturbance. It is time consuming and emotionally exhausting. The negotiation, the due diligence and the continual visits by inquisitive strangers take over your working day and keep you awake at night. If you are not careful, the well being of your business and your health will suffer. Concentrating on selling the business can be so distracting that owners forget that they still have a business to run. An end of term attitude sets in. The personal items have already been packed ready to go. Nothing matters now; the business is sold and the new owners will be here shortly to take charge of everything. Thinking like this after you have struck a deal to sell is a big mistake and can lead to problems.

Finalising the sale of your business may take several months and neglecting the day-to-day running of it now can have serious consequences.

During this period beware, the buyer is watching.

The initial sale negotiation was based on information that you provided but, during the due diligence the buyer will be looking for reassurance that your business is really performing as it was portrayed. His auditor will be asking for management reports and posing questions about current trading activity. How are this month's sales figures looking? Is the business on target to meet the projections you provided? Are profit margins holding up? Are any of your employees aware of what is happening and are they all happy?

At this delicate stage of the process, a fall in sales or profitability will raise doubts in the buyer's mind about the strength of the whole proposition. If profit falls, the potential value of your business falls in direct proportion. There may be a simple explanation for the setback but a nervous buyer can react by lowering the price offered or, even worse, decide that there is something wrong with your sums and withdraw his offer.

The deal you have agreed is still very delicate and can be easily damaged. You do not want to give the buyer any reason to change his mind so you need to run the business very carefully to avoid wasting the hard work you have already done.

You must keep staff motivated.

Exit Strategy

If your employees find out that you are selling as a result of a premature announcement or a leak, you will have problems. You may want to tell the world that you are leaving but your staff still need to feel their jobs are secure, confident that they have a future and, importantly, that they are valued, important members of a team.

Take the case of a Sales Manager who suddenly hears from his Managing Director that the company has been sold. The manager runs the entire marketing operation and is a key worker but he had no idea that the owner was thinking of selling up. He asks the identity of the new owners and what their plans are only to be told by his boss that the information is still confidential. Uncertain about his prospects, the Sales Manager wonders if he is going to lose his job. Maybe the new owners have a sales operation of their own and don't need him. How is he going to pay the mortgage and the loan on the new car? What will his wife say? Inevitably, he discusses the news with colleagues. Morale plummets, affecting company performance. The Sales Manager feels hurt and let down. It is time to do something about the betrayal and he decides to act. He quickly finds another job with a competitor eager to take him and his knowledge. It is only when the Sales Manager hands in his resignation that his employer realises the seriousness of his mistake. He has been insensitive and foolish but it is too late; the damage has been done. He wonders if anyone else is job hunting and how the buyer will react when he finds out.

Ironically, the main reasons the new owners are buying the company is to acquire its excellent marketing department and the good reputation of the business. They want to expand and give everyone the opportunity to grow with the business. They even see the Sales Manager as a potential Managing Director capable of running the company for them. Sadly, because the buyer's plans had not been discussed with the retiring owner, he knew nothing about any of this.

To avoid this type of damaging development the seller must continue managing his employees carefully right up until the day when responsibility passes and the new owner takes over.

Continue to use cover stories to explain the strange visitors and strictly maintain confidentiality. Take care to keep your staff unaware that things are about to change. Announcements will come later when the new owner has arrived. The new employer is the only person that can reassure staff and convince them that they will be looked after in the future.

You may think that saying nothing about the sale of the business a secret is enough to keep your company at its pcak performance. It isn't! Your attitude and demeanour can also reveal that something is happening. Change the way you work, your attitude or your manner and employees will quickly recognize that something is going on. Changes breed uncertainty. Take your eye off the ball and your workers will do the same. They will know that, for some reason, you no longer care and if you no longer care why should they? Check that your routines are the same as before. If you always held weekly meeting, keep having them and remember that you still need show that the business excites you. Even if you don't feel excited any longer, fake it.

In some circumstances there may be key employees who will have to know what is going on before the deal is finalised. Discuss the situation with the buyer before bringing anyone in on your secret and work out the best way to involve them. Generally speaking, the fewer people that know anything the better and anyone who is told must be made fully aware of their responsibility to keep quiet.

It's a good idea to take the stress home.

One way to reduce nasty surprises in the office is to arrange for email correspondence about the transaction to go to your home email address. Some questions, particularly during the due diligence, can be quite stressful and reading them at home, when you are alone, gives you time to calm down and control your emotions well away from any employees. Taking the stress out of the office reduces the chance of staff wondering why you are red in the face or angry for no apparent reason.

Have a cover story ready.

Despite your best efforts, there is still a danger that someone will learn or suspect you are selling the business. A private letter may accidentally get opened, a phone call or conversation overheard or an email sent to the wrong person. That person may confront you and ask if it is true or you may hear rumours have started. You need to have a plausible explanation ready in advance to cover this situation. It may be appropriate to say that you are talking to another company about a joint marketing venture or manufacturing for them. Another possibility is to say that they are considering investing to enable you to expand the business and their accountants are checking things out first.

It is usually possible to take the facts that have come to light and make them part of a good news story. The important thing is to contain any gossip quickly and explain what has been discovered in a positive manner. Preparing a suitable tale beforehand gives you more time to think of a good cover and make it believable. A prepared cover story will enable you to deal with any leak confidently and is more likely to work than making something up on the spur of the moment or just denying everything.

No isn't the time to make structural changes.

In the company profile, your buyer was offered a proposition based on a particular business model. He is buying the company you offered him. Change the shape of the business and it may become less attractive to him. Once a provisional offer has been made you should not restructure or change the nature of the business. No buyer wants to buy a company only to find it has become something different in the last three months. Before selling the business you may have planned to take on more staff, launch a costly marketing campaign or buy a new factory but now is not the time to start any of these projects. Making changes can also increase overheads and reduce profit, alarming the buyer before he has completed the deal.

Your buyer will expect the business to be in a stable condition when he arrives and will have his own plans for changing it in the future. By then the company will not be your responsibility and you will not be thanked for making unnecessary changes that become irrelevant or unwanted.

Avoid going for short-term gains.

While a price for your business may have been agreed in principle, it can still vary even when there are no further price negotiations. The price actually paid for the business will be calculated after final accounts are completed. These accounts, similar to year-end accounts, are done after the final sale agreement is signed. One element affecting the price is the performance of the business between signing the heads of agreement and the completion of the deal. It is the last time, assuming the sale goes through, that you are in control of the company and an opportunity to try and drive the business hard to generate some extra profit. It sounds a tempting proposition since as well as pushing up the price you are leaving on a high note. While profit generated during this period may get added to the price, it is not always a good idea to sacrifice prudent management for short-term gain.

A quick increase in net margin can be achieved by cutting overheads. Long-term expenditure cut from the profit and loss account will not affect sales and pruning items like product development, plant maintenance or support staff levels will quickly improve net margins. Raising prices will also directly increase profitability. The idea may be appealing but most buyers will be watching for this type of activity and unhappy if they come across it. Making such poor management decisions can have a detrimental effect on the business in the long run. Just as a fall off in performance during due diligence will concern the buyer a sudden rise in sales or margins will cause questions to be asked.

Chopping overheads to generate a short-term gain carries an additional risk. If the deal collapses, you are the one left to pick up the pieces and get the business back on track.

In effect you have become a caretaker.

While the due diligence and final negotiations are continuing you should operate the business as if you are a temporary custodian or interim manager, intent on keeping each part of the operation functioning properly and handing the company on to the new owner with everything operating smoothly. As a caretaker, you need to keep the business working at its best, without taking any unnecessary risks.

10 *It's a contract, Jim, but not as we know it.*

The movie mogul, Samuel Goldwyn is reputed to have said, 'A verbal contract isn't worth the paper it's written on.' A view that applies equally to the deal you are negotiating.

While the buyer is carrying out due diligence his lawyer is preparing the first draft of the contract, the document that will be the basis of the completed deal. The contract also known as the 'Purchase Agreement' or 'Share Sale Agreement' takes the key points from the heads of terms and adds additional clauses to clarify exactly what the transaction involves.

When a business changes hands, the seller leaves with money and the buyer gets the business. Having parted with his cash, the buyer is vulnerable since the business may be faulty or have been misrepresented in some way. The buyer's lawyer writes the first draft because most of the document is designed to protect the buyer's position in the event of something going wrong with the deal. Going first gives the buyer an opportunity to insert defensive clauses, add conditions not previously negotiated and generally write the contract to his advantage. The weapons the buyer uses to draft the contract are an array of guarantees, warranties and indemnities all of which are designed to move risk from the buyer back to the seller.

The ideal contract from the buyer's perspective is one where the seller guarantees everything both now and in the future so there is no risk involved in buying the company. The seller, however, would want a contract where he took the money and left with no potential future liability, *(caveat emptor)* – let the buyer beware. As a result of the differences in position it is not surprising that the seller normally rejects the first draft and it is common for the contract to undergo vigorous negotiation before it is agreed. Revised drafts are passed between both sets of lawyers many times until everyone accepts the final version. Once again, email and change tracking software have made the process easier and faster.

So what is the structure of a share sale agreement?

A typical share sale agreement may be laid out as follows. I've included the twelve that applied to the sale of my company but they may vary: -

First come Definitions and Interpretations
Sets out who the contract is between, statutory details of the business being sold and the amount being paid.

Exit Strategy

This is followed by a glossary of key words and phrases together with the precise meanings they are to have in the agreement.

Second Agreement for sale
Details how the business is being sold e.g. shares in exchange for money, (A cash consideration) or shares in exchange for stock in the buying company.

Third Consideration
The amount being paid broken down to detail at what point different payments are made e.g. when stage payments are to be made.

Forth comes Completion
Confirms where the completion meeting will take place, what other documents need to be produced and the legal process that will occur to transfer the business to the new owners. The completion meeting is normally held at the buyer's lawyer's offices.

Fifth Completion accounts
These clauses details which accountants will prepare the completion accounts for the business, how long they have to prepare the accounts and the reporting method to be used. Completion accounts clauses can also state the dispute procedure that will operate if there is any disagreement regarding the final figures.

Sixth Escrow Account
An interest bearing bank account where an agreed sum of money is held jointly, usually by both sets of lawyers. The escrow money stays available to be used to compensate the buyer in the event of a successful claim against the seller. Details of the escrow account

will include the amount of time the buyer has a to make a claim. After that time has expired - the cut off date - the money is passed to the seller together with any accrued interest.

Seventh Warranties and Representations by the Vendor

It is here that the buyer inserts the items he wants you to warrant. Warranties and covenants are the promises that you are making as part of the sales of the business and these clauses describe the circumstances allowing the buyer to make a claim for damages.

Eighth the Tax Covenant

In these clauses the buyer will require promises that you will pay any tax liabilities that have been incurred before he bought the business. It covers all forms of taxation and includes taxes where no liability has yet been found.

Ninth Restrictive covenants

Details any restrictions placed on the seller stopping you from competing with the company you have sold e.g. approaching staff to offer them employment or using knowledge owned by the business.

Tenth Pensions

The pension clauses set out how existing pension arrangements will be dealt with as the business changes hands.

Eleventh General

Covers who pays what professional fees, who controls any announcements about the sale of the business and other standards terms.

Exit Strategy

And finally twelfth Notices

Notices clauses detail how the buyer and seller notify each other of disputes or claims arising later.

Attached to the agreement will be a series of schedules detailing the company and its assets together with the detailed list of warranties and tax covenants you are undertaking plus a schedule of vendor protection.

Because of the nature of the agreement, its primary purpose being to protect the buyer; the warranty and covenant details are likely to be the largest parts of the document. The last schedule, vendor protection, includes clauses designed to benefit the vendor in the event of a dispute. These can include setting an upper limit on the total amount claimed, a lower limit to stop unreasonably small or silly claims, a time limit after which the buyer can no longer make a claim and a right of reasonable access to documentation, premises and staff for the seller if there is a claim.

It's important to understand the jargon.

A share sale agreement is an intimidating document. Even where the transaction is uncomplicated, the contract can be 90 to 100 pages long. It will contain a lot of words and phrases with which you are not familiar. Before you sign the contract it is essential that you understand the implications of every word and every clause. The contract is legally binding and you should not rely on your lawyer to say a point is acceptable if you do not understand what it means.

You need a meeting with your lawyer and agent to examine the draft contract. Work slowly through the document, asking for an explanation of each clause and its implications. Asking why the buyer has inserted a clause can help to explain its meaning. Many clauses will need amending and your lawyer will need you to tell him which risks you are prepared to live with and which are unacceptable.

An example might be a buyer who includes the following warranty clause in the draft agreement regarding the equipment owned by the company: -

'The plant, machinery, vehicles and other equipment employed for the business of the company is capable, and will remain capable of doing the work it was purchased for until it has been written down to nil value in the company accounts.'

This warranty that you are being asked to give sounds harmless enough. Why shouldn't the buyer expect the machinery to carry on working? You know that the plant, vehicles and other equipment are working perfectly well at the moment, but are you prepared to give the undertaking the buyer is asking for? Depreciating equipment on a reducing balance takes many years. Can you be sure it will carry on working for that length of time? You will not be maintaining the equipment and have no control over how it will be treated. What does '*other equipment*' include? Computers frequently become obsolete before they are written off. Technology moves forwards quickly making hardware and software redundant long before they are depreciated down to nothing. Are you really prepared to warrant that vehicles will last until they are written off in the accounts?

The wording of the warranty the buyer has included is strong. It makes it possible for him to make a claim for damages against you if any of these items became uneconomic to repair before they are fully depreciated. In effect, you are accepting the future responsibility for all the equipment in the company, a commercial risk that the buyer should be taking on himself. By drafting this clause the buyer has tried to move the risk from himself onto you.

You may decide it is an unreasonable warranty and refuse to accept it. One way would be to reject the warranty, out of hand, as unfair and propose that the buyer arranges for an inspection, at his expense, of the plant, machinery, vehicles and other equipment. That way he can satisfy himself about its suitability for use in the company. Another option is to ask that the warranty be modified to read: -

'The plant, machinery, vehicles and other equipment employed for the business of the company are not unsafe, uneconomical or obsolete and do not require replacement.'

Changing to this wording gives the buyer some comfort that the machinery and plant is working properly at the present time when you are selling it. However, it does not make any promises about future performance and avoids lumbering you with a potential liability that you cannot quantify or control.

A share sale agreement for an uncomplicated business sale can contain something like 600 clauses. Many will be straightforward but a considerable number will be contentious and require changing or removing. During the contract negotiations it is not uncommon for the buyer to introduce additional clauses designed to protect against something his due diligence has revealed. It's unrealistic to refuse to give any warranties and a buyer would quickly suspect something if you did. One example you will not escape is tax covenants. These are the clauses where you indemnify the buyer against tax liabilities that have occurred before he took over the business. Your covenant to pay any outstanding tax that may be discovered later removes the risk of a surprise tax bill for the new owner. Why should the new owner of the business pay for a mistake you have previously made in a vat return, an underpayment of PAYE or an incorrect corporation tax calculation? A covenant to pay any outstanding tax due is expected and reasonable to give.

As each revision is returned to your lawyer he will make proposals for amendments and forward the document on to you, usually by email, asking for your instruction on the different points being altered. As with due diligence, it is a good idea to get the draft contracts sent to your home email address. You need peace, quiet and a clear head to interpret and understand the alterations.

Just as the buyer may be discovering things during due diligence that he wants to protect himself from, you may find clauses in the share sale agreement that give cause for concern and remind you of something that you really should tell the buyer about.

There will almost certainly be a clause something like this: -

'There is nothing affecting the company that we have not disclosed in writing to the buyer or his lawyer which if disclosed might alter the decision of the buyer to enter into this share sale agreement.'

It is a catch-all warranty and a safety net for the buyer in case he has forgotten to cover any potential issue that may be a threat to the business. The safest and simplest answer is to disclose everything even if you doubt its relevance or importance. Let the buyer judge if an issue is important. If it isn't, he can ignore it. The important point for the seller, however, is that once the buyer knows about something, he cannot return to it later after he has purchased your company and complain. By accepting your disclosure, the buyer is making what you have told him part of the contract.

Sometimes other lines of communication can be useful.

Re-drafting the contract involves a considerable amount of negotiation. Because of the need for tight and precise wording, most of the work will be done through the lawyers but you still have other lines of communication that you may need to use. Take the situation where a buyer is demanding a condition that is unreasonable and you are unable to concede. The lawyer on the other side has his instructions and is standing firm. Your lawyer has hit a brick wall. If this happens, ask your agent to talk to the buyer's advisor. He can explain your problem and suggest the advisor discusses the obstacle with the buyer. After such an approach, sending your agent through the side door, a buyer will often modify his position allowing a compromise to be reached. The lawyers can redraft or remove the offending clause and move on. Depending on the relationship you have developed with the buyer it may be appropriate to talk to him yourself but be careful - positions can quickly become entrenched if the conversation goes wrong.

The thing to remember is that creating contracts is an industry.

The size and complexity of the legal documents relating to the sale of a company make them time consuming to prepare. There is an almost daily stream of new case law creating the need for revisions of clauses and the restructuring of documents. Even as you listen to this audio book things will have changed. Our government is continually passing new legislation affecting how companies operate and the responsibilities of director and owners. European burcaucrats are also creating red tape adding to the issues demanding a buyer's attention before he buys a company. Recent topical examples like environmental protection and employment discrimination law have the potential to cost a business thousands of pounds in fines or compensation. In future, as the jobsworths create even more regulations, buyers will be asking for warranties to protect against these new rules. Inevitably, due diligence and share sale agreements will get bigger as each new threat is recognised.

Exit Strategy

The need to keep up with the increasingly rapid rate of change has made many corporate lawyers subscribe to a document service where an outside legal firm provides draft paperwork for use under licence. The providers have the resources to make sure their documents are kept up to date with current case law and legislation, something only a large law practice would be able to do in-house. To make the job easier for the lawyer, the legal draft comes complete with two sets of guidance notes, one set of instructions for modifying the agreement if you are acting for the buyer and a different set for the vendor's lawyer. The development of the internet has helped this service to flourish enabling legal firms to save time, control costs and increase margins.

It may sound like a cosy gravy train but the risks the lawyer is protecting you from is real. A well-negotiated agreement can make a big difference to the outcome of the sale, particularly when things go wrong. If there is a disagreement later it will become apparent that the devil really is in the detail. Fortunately, serious disputes, once the sale has been completed, are rare and most share sale agreements never get looked at again.

Graham Watkins

11   We meet at dusk.

When J.R.R. Tolkein wrote, 'A star shone at the hour of our meeting.' he was writing fiction but, strangely, most completion meetings take place late in the day.

The due diligence is completed and the final wording of the share sale agreement has just about been agreed. Until now, all the work that has been done has been speculative. Either party is still able to walk away from the deal leaving the other side paying some hefty bills and wondering where they went wrong. All that is about to change. It is time to complete the sale.

It's time for the completion meeting.

Completing the sale commits the buyer and the seller to the transaction and everyone involved in the deal normally attends the meeting when this happens.

During the meeting, the share sale agreement is signed by the buyer and the seller, the due diligence documents are formally exchanged, ownership of the business transfers to the buyer and the seller is paid. It sounds simple but a large amount of paperwork is involved.

Unlike the negotiation meeting when the seller organised the venue, this meeting is usually held at the offices of the lawyers acting for the buyer. This is not intended to be a negotiating meeting and there is no need for neutral ground. In addition, there are practical advantages in holding the meeting in the lawyers' premises. Law firms conducting this type of work have suitable rooms able to accommodate the number of people that need to attend. Sometimes more than one area is needed so that the buyer can conclude arrangements with his financers in private while the seller's team are in another room. With bigger deals several meeting may need to go on simultaneously.

Another benefit of using the lawyers' office is the availability of legal secretarial staff to act in support. During the meeting, things get changed and documents need to be rewritten and copied. The hosting lawyers will normally coordinate the documentation needed for the meeting. With the meeting taking place in the office, copies are available as computer files. This makes the job of amending and reprinting as required easier.

Here's a peculiar thing.
For some reason, which has never been explained to me, most completion meetings start late in the

afternoon and continue until very late in the evening. Hit a few snags and you can find yourself still arguing with the buyer in the early hours of the morning. Someone has even suggested that the lawyers who specialise in handling business sales are like vampires. They prefer to appear and do their work at night. This is a rather unkind comment and probably made by a seller who did not negotiate a fixed fee with his lawyer. It is sensible not to add up the hourly fees of all the lawyers and advisors present at the completion unless you have fixed your costs or want to be upset. By all means bring a bottle of champagne to celebrate but think about including a sleeping bag and be ready for a long night.

The completion meeting can be a stressful climax.

Unless you have been involved in a completion meeting before you will be unsure of how the meeting will work. Most sellers only experience one completion meeting in their life and find the experience confusing. You are at the climax of months of preparation and hard work. For the first time, the exit sign is in plain view. You are about to part with the business that has been a major part of your life. The act of signing away your company is an emotional occurrence, a tipping point after which your life changes dramatically. In the few hours during the meeting a lot of things will happen very quickly. The exit sign may be illuminated but there is still time for something to go wrong and mess up the deal.

Reduce the risk of a last second foul up by making sure that you are properly prepared before you go to the completion meeting. Your role is an active one and although your lawyer will guide you through the technicalities, there are things you need to do in advance.

Get your paperwork ready.

The buyer's team will be coordinating the documents needed to complete the sale but there is paperwork that you are required to bring to the meeting. Some will be listed in the share sale agreement. As the sale progresses, you will be expected to hand them over to the new owners. Ask you lawyer for an itemised list of the documents you need to produce and gather them together ready to take with you.

Examples that are specified might include: -

Signed and completed share transfer forms.
The certificate of incorporation of the company.
The statutory books for the company.
Company seal.
Title deeds relating to properties owned by the company.
Chequebooks, paying in books and credit cards owned by the company.
Bank certificates confirming closing balances of accounts.
A letter from the bank releasing the company from all guarantees and charges.
A letter of resignation from the company's auditors.
Your letter of resignation as a director, in an agreed form.
A deed releasing the company from any claim from the seller.

Exit Strategy

Making sure that you take everything that is needed is important. Collecting the paperwork together can take time and turning up without key documents may stop the deal being completed. As well as taking specified papers, it might be appropriate to include keys for company premises, a list of alarm and door entry codes and the phone numbers of key holders. If you are driving to the meeting in a car owned by the company, think about how you are going to get home. The buyer may demand the car keys and you cannot rely on buses in the early hours of the morning.

A lot will be happening on the day of the completion meeting.

There is a lot of activity during the day of a completion meeting. Lawyers are finalising and printing documents. There is an urgency to make sure everything is ready on time. The phones are busy and emails fly about confirming agreement on changes. It is a frantic race to avoid postponing and everyone is getting excited. Closing the sale of a business is a big deal even for the professionals involved. It's what they have been building up to for months.

Before the completion meeting starts, the buyer will sit down with his team and go over everything one last time. You should be doing the same. Ask your lawyer to explain what is going to happen during the completion. If he is struggling to make time, one way may be to travel to the meeting together, giving you the opportunity to talk in the car. Knowing the order of events and how the completion will be conducted will increase your confidence and lower your stress level. Make the mistake of turning up with no idea about how things are done and you will look and behave like a startled rabbit. Your lawyer will lead you but you still need to understand what is happening.

An agenda for a completion meeting might read like this: -

1 The vendor shall deliver to the purchaser.

Completed and signed transfers in favour of the purchaser in respect of the shares together with related share certificates.

Waivers, consents or other documents required to give good title of the shares and enable the purchaser to be registered as the holder of the shares.

Statutory books, certificates of incorporation, company seal and all chequebooks and credit cards held by the vendor.

Certificates of the amounts outstanding for each bank account. A deed confirming the directors are retiring.

A deed releasing the company from any liability to the vendor or any third party.

A discharge of the company for all bank guarantees.

The resignation of the company auditors.

2 Directors loans

Exit Strategy

The vendors will repay any money they owe the company.

3 A board meeting of the company shall be held at which

A resolution shall be passed to register the transfer of the shares and to register, in the register of members, the purchaser as the holder of the shares.

There shall be appointed as directors and secretary such persons as the purchaser may nominate.

The outgoing directors resignations will be tendered and accepted.

All existing bank authorities shall be revoked and replaced with new bank authorities.

The registered office of the company shall be changed to an address decided by the purchaser.

The company's auditors resignation shall be accepted and new auditors appointed by the purchaser.

4 After full completion of items 1 to 3 the purchaser will

Pay the completion payment as specified in the share sale agreement.

Pay the retention payment to the escrow account holders as specified in the share sale agreement.

Reading the agenda makes the completion meeting sound straight forward and rather boring. It can be, but the purpose of having this meeting involving the lawyers is to make sure that everything has been done correctly and in the right order.

The trick is to make it a formality.

Things do not always go according to plan and completion meetings can go awry. Important documents may be missing causing moments of high drama. A mistake spotted in the contract can cause frantic rewriting and arguing by the lawyers. The buyer may suddenly realise that he has misunderstood a significant clause, threatening the outcome. It has even been known for the buyer and seller to give up and withdraw to the pub, leaving their legal teams at loggerheads over the wording of some arcane clause.

Ideally, you need the completion meeting to run smoothly, like clockwork, with documents being signed, resolutions passed and matters taking their natural course without any fuss. By making sure everything is right beforehand the completion meeting becomes a mere formality. The buyer is given no reason or excuse to back out.

Finally it's time to grin.

As the meeting progresses a large pile of paperwork will move steadily from one side of the table to the other and at some point the lawyers and advisers will start to grin at their clients. If it is your first completion you will wonder why but the answer is a simple one and you did not even notice. You have just sold your company and are looking across the table at the new owners. There is no going back. Almost everything is settled.

Of course at this point I asked a direct question, 'Where is the money?'

While everyone is shaking hands and glasses are being filled with champagne, you remember something important that seems to have been forgotten. The buyer has not paid you any money. These days it is very unlikely that a buyer would turn up at a completion meeting with a suitcase full of cash. If he did, the taxman would be asking why and you would have to watch out for muggers on the way home. So where is it?

Before the meeting, the buyer will have transferred the money to his lawyer's client account and it sits there, as cleared funds, ready for paying to you when the deal is completed. However, since most deals are concluded at night, outside bank opening hours, it is impossible to transfer the money simultaneously with completion of the deal.

To get around the problem, the buyer's lawyer hands your lawyer a letter confirming that he has the money on deposit and giving an undertaking that he will transfer it, usually electronically, as soon as the banks are open for business. If that is the next day, don't forget to ask for the overnight interest. After all, it is your money he is holding. Considering all the complications the lawyers have introduced into the sale of your company, this may seem a very gentlemanly and laid-back way to handle the money, but that is how they do it.

The significance of what has just happened will not have sunk in as you drive home. You whole life has just changed. A long holiday might be the next thing on your agenda but there are still a couple of jobs to be taken care of before you see the last of the company you used to own.

12   Riding into the sunset.

The great story teller and film producer Orson Welles once said, 'If you want a happy ending, that depends of course, on where you stop your story.' And here you are at the end of your story.

All the planning and hard work has paid off. You have successfully sold your company. The pressure of keeping secrets from your employees, running the business and negotiating your exit is over. A great weight has just lifted from your shoulders and your emotions will be mixed. You will feel tired, euphoric, confused and lost. The time has come to get away, recharge you batteries and collect your thoughts ready for your next project. Before you do however, there are still some issues relating to the business that have to be dealt with.

First there are some announcements.

One of the first things that need to be done is to tell the staff and possibly the media that the business has changed hands. Employees will be anxious to meet the new owner. The purchaser will want to control how announcements are made so that the company image he wants is projected. Who has responsibility for making the deal public knowledge can be a condition in the contract and the wording of press releases or announcements is usually settled during the completion meeting. Employees will need to be told with sensitivity and the new owner may ask you to take part by introducing him and helping to explain the positive aspects of the business transfer. To have a smooth changeover, the employees need reassuring that they have nothing to fear. Before you tell anyone that the business has been sold, ask the new owner how he wants you to conduct yourself. He is the boss and your role is a minor supporting one.

Are there any consultancy agreements?

During the completion meeting you may have entered into a consultancy agreement with the company. The purpose of the consultancy is to enable the new owner to call on you for information to help him take over the running of the business smoothly. He may ask you to introduce him to key suppliers and produce background information that he can use in the future or, faced with a problem, ask how you would have dealt with the same issue in the past.

A consultant works on a self-employed basis and you are not an employee of the company. This will cause some confusion until people adjust to the idea that you are no longer in charge. If someone comes to you for an answer, refer him straight to the new owner, a difficult thing to do if you are a leader used to taking action and making quick decisions.

The new owner will want your knowledge but at the same time you will quickly realise that you are, like the ghost of Christmas past, in the way. Having bought your company, the purchaser will want you off the premises as soon as possible. Before long he is likely to suggest that he calls you into the office when he needs you. It's nothing personal. He needs you out of the way because you are a distraction. If it happens, enjoy the gardening leave.

Then there will be a stocktaking.

Although the details of the sale have been settled there is still some accounting work to be done before everything is finalised. A stock valuation needs to be arrived at and a stock take is necessary. This may be done the day after the completion meeting or possibly before with adjustments being made for any stock movements that have taken place. Checking the stock is a one off and cannot be redone later on if a mistake has been made. Because of this and the importance of the stock-take, it can directly influence the price being paid for the business; both the buyer and the seller are normally involved.

Next come the completion accounts.

Following the stock-take, the auditors prepare a set of accounts valuing the business at the time of completion.

Completion accounts are similar to financial year-end accounts but they are not always prepared in the same way. The accounting report used in a business sale is a private document produced purely for the transaction. It is not filed at Company House and different accounting practices, set out in the share sale agreement, can be used to arrive at values. For example, an asset may be valued at a cost price ignoring depreciation increasing its value or slow moving and obsolete stock may be written down to nil value. Changing the way values are arrived at alters the value of the company for the purposes of the deal and details of how the completion accounts are prepared will have been negotiated earlier.

The share sale agreement sets out who is responsible for producing these completion accounts and how long they are allowed to complete the work. The buyer's auditor normally undertakes this job but not always. The purchaser may be willing for your side to prepare the completion accounts if his accountant cannot finish the job in time or is inexperienced in producing this type of accounting report. You gain an advantage when your side get the opportunity to produce the figures particularly if your accountant has been acting as your advisor or agent. If he has, he will already be familiar with all the issues and able to present a set of figures that are favourable to your position.

Once the completion accounts have been produced, they are delivered to the other side's accountants together with all supporting calculations. A set time is allowed for the figures to be checked and any objection to be made to the final valuation of the

Exit Strategy

business. Time is of the essence and once the deadline for objecting has passed, the accounts are automatically accepted as correct. Where an objection has been made before the deadline and the accountants cannot be agreed, the share sale agreement lays out a dispute procedure; usually an independent accountant to act as an arbitrator.

Preparation and approval of the completion account is an important element of the sales process. The price you get will depend on it. Buyers include clauses in the contract linking the price they will pay for the business to the net asset value. Tying the two together protects the buyer from the seller stripping value out of the business just before he sells it. The share sale agreement will say something like: -

'If the net assets shown by the completion account are less than £x the shortfall defined as the asset deficit the consideration shall be reduced by an amount equal to the asset deficit.'

With this clause in the share sale agreement, a buyer can reduce the amount paid in direct proportion to any reduction in value of the company. A consequence of the clause is that the final price will vary. The value of the business may have fallen because of a poor trading period during the negotiation or some other loss. It is a reasonable position since any loss will have occurred while you were still running the business.

If there is an asset deficit, the buyer makes a claim and the difference is returned to him from the escrow account. Your liability does not end with the money held in the escrow account. Where the deficit is larger than the amount held in escrow, the buyer is entitled to claim any outstanding balance back from you.

Linking the price being paid for the business to the net asset value can give the seller an opportunity to increase the price by having a profitable trading period in the run up to completion. For the seller to benefit, the clause should include wording confirming that the price does increase in proportion to any increase in asset value. Without this part of the clause the buyer can just keep the additional value you have generated and pay nothing extra for it. The alternative, but probably less tax efficient option, is for you to take out any extra profit generated before completion leaving the net value of the business at the sum agreed on the contract.

In practice, both sides will have done their own sums before signing the deal and final figures usually come close to expectations.

Now all you have to do is honour your obligations and wait.

Once the completion accounts have been agreed there is very little else that you need to do. The warranties and covenants that you have given in the share sale agreement will apply until they expire - usually in two or three years. During that time the buyer can still claim damages for any breach of the agreement that you commit or any fault he finds in the business that was not disclosed. Finally, the guarantees you have given expire and it's all over. If there has been no claim, you have no further liability to the new owner of the business.

What next you may wonder?

After the excitement had died away you may feel a loss of status and a sense of disappointment. By removing the stress you have created a lack of inertia. A common reaction is to try and get straight back in the game. Buying a business on the rebound is usually a mistake. Unless your exit strategy included starting again, don't rush into anything. Why risk replacing the great company you have built up and sold with one that may never succeed. Have that long holiday you always wanted and remember the phone won't ring with a problem at work. Later, when you have regained your equilibrium and taken stock of your new situation, is the time to start thinking about the next project. But that, of course, is another story.

Graham Watkins

Exit Strategy

Other books by Graham Watkins include;

The Sicilian Defence
The Iron Masters
A White Man's War
The Welsh Folly book
Welsh Legends and Myths
Birth of a Salesman

You might also be interested in 'How to Sell Ice to Eskimos' a book explaining the selling tips and techniques Graham has used during the last forty years. They are effective and helped turn him from a novice into a top rate closer of deals.

Come and visit Graham's website to see what's new.
www.grahamwatkins.info

Graham Watkins

About the Author

After training as a marine engineer, Graham followed a successful career in sales and marketing until 1989 when he incorporated his own company, distributing retail and catering equipment.

The company grew and was sold in 2003 but the experience of dealing with the sale of the business made him realise how poorly prepared he was to make the most of the business which was his biggest asset. There was virtually nothing written to explain how to sell a company and the books that were available were mainly textbooks, written by accountants or lawyers.

Retired from business, he now lives with my wife in a rambling farmhouse in the Brecon Beacons and enjoys life, hobby-farming and writing.

Made in the USA
Lexington, KY
15 March 2018